BUDDHISM

Real-life Buddhist Teachings & Practices for Real Change

(A Guide to Start Practicing Buddhist Meditation)

Viola Hansen

Published by Oliver Leish

Viola Hansen

All Rights Reserved

Buddhism: Real-life Buddhist Teachings & Practices for Real Change (A Guide to Start Practicing Buddhist Meditation)

ISBN 978-1-77485-187-6

All rights reserved. No part of this guide may be reproduced in any form without permission in writing from the publisher except in the case of brief quotations embodied in critical articles or reviews.

Legal & Disclaimer

The information contained in this book is not designed to replace or take the place of any form of medicine or professional medical advice. The information in this book has been provided for educational and entertainment purposes only.

The information contained in this book has been compiled from sources deemed reliable, and it is accurate to the best of the Author's knowledge; however, the Author cannot guarantee its accuracy and validity and cannot be held liable for any errors or omissions. Changes are periodically made to this book. You must consult your doctor or get professional medical advice before using any of the suggested remedies, techniques, or information in this book.

Upon using the information contained in this book, you agree to hold harmless the Author from and against any damages, costs, and expenses, including any legal fees potentially resulting from the application of any of the information provided by this guide. This disclaimer applies to any damages or injury caused by the use and application, whether directly or indirectly, of any advice or information presented, whether for breach of contract, tort, negligence, personal injury, criminal intent, or under any other cause of action.

You agree to accept all risks of using the information presented inside this book. You need to consult a professional medical practitioner in order to ensure you are both able and healthy enough to participate in this program.

TABLE OF CONTENTS

INTRODUCTION 1

CHAPTER 1: WHAT IS BUDDHISM? 4

CHAPTER 2: BUDDHISM 10

CHAPTER 3: THE TEACHINGS OF BUDDHISM 15

CHAPTER 4: HOW TO HAVE THE RIGHT ACTION, RIGHT LIFE, AND RIGHT EFFORT 33

CHAPTER 5: THE EIGHTFOLD PATH 36

CHAPTER 6: WALKING TOWARDS AWAKENING: LEARNING THE PATH 42

CHAPTER 7: THE BELIEF SYSTEMS 47

CHAPTER 8: THE TWINS KNOWN AS ENLIGHTENMENT AND DARKNESS 51

CHAPTER 9: HAPPINESS DOESN'T DEPEND ON WHAT YOU HAVE OR WHO YOU ARE. IT ALL DEPENDS ON WHAT YOU THINK" - BUDDHA 57

CHAPTER 10: MINDFULNESS 66

CHAPTER 11: THE BELIEFS THAT UNDERLIE BUDDHISM ... 70

CHAPTER 12: HOW THE IMPERMANENT CAUSES US PAIN AND HOW TO AVOID IT 81

CHAPTER 13: THE EIGHT FOLD PATH TO TRUE HAPPINESS 86

CHAPTER 14: THE ROAD TO VICTORY 93

CHAPTER 15: MEDITATION	**116**
CHAPTER 16: SYMBOLISM	**125**
CHAPTER 17: THE SOURCE OF HAPPINESS	**132**
CHAPTER 18: PROMINENT BUDDHIST FIGURES	**143**
CHAPTER 19: MINDFULNESS	**155**
CHAPTER 20: FOUR NOBLE TRUTHS	**159**
CHAPTER 21: NOBLE TRUTHS AND HOW TO INTERPRET THEM	**165**
CONCLUSION	**177**

Introduction

Did you know that Buddhism is now more popular than it was in the last century? It is evident by the increase in Buddhist and Yoga books and the expansion of Yoga schools around the world.

You might have even seen more people - film stars, competitors, mogul head honchos, and your next-door neighbor - who are incorporating Buddhist practices into their daily lives.

However, many of the questions about Buddhism remain unanswered. Is it a religion that has its own set of rules? Is it a lighter-hearted way of living? Is resurrection possible? Is karma like destiny?

This book is for you if you're interested in learning more about Buddhism, particularly how to get rid of stress and uneasiness. It is a well-known fact that

Buddhism is an amazing theme. The seed that the First Buddha planted three thousand years ago is still a huge tree that continues to grow right up until the present.

This book will help you to create a foundation for learning and honing Buddhism. Tenderfoots can ask many questions, such as what Buddhism is and its lessons. The unmistakable depiction of the center subjects, such as the Four Noble Truths or the Noble Eightfold Path, is striking.

In a clear and concise manner, Buddhist concepts such as Nirvana and Reincarnation are also clarified. You will also learn the practical side of Buddhism to help you achieve peace and unwind every day, hypotheses aside.

This book is intended for all people who are interested in Buddhism. It is especially for those who want to use it as a guide for living a happy and intentional life. The decision is now yours. Clear away the confusion and begin your journey to true serenity, clarity and peace. The main Chapter is waiting!

Chapter 1: What is Buddhism?

You won't be able to see beyond the saffron robes or meditating monks no matter how many spirituality books you have read. You don't need to read a lot of books, listen to long lectures and attend boring seminars to truly understand Buddhism. It's not like learning math. It doesn't require you to memorize any formulas to solve problems. You only need an open mind.

An ancient Zen legend tells of a Japanese professor visiting a Japanese master to learn Zen. The host served tea to his guest, but didn't stop pouring until the cup was full. The professor looked at him and said, "My cup is full." It is impossible to fill it with more tea. The Japanese master stopped pouring the tea and said to the professor: "Just as this cup, your head also full." It is full your thoughts, ideas, and limited thinking. You will never truly grasp Zen. There are no words or things I can say. What can I teach you if your cup isn't full?

My question is: "How can I understand Buddhism if I don't empty my cup first?" You won't find the answers to your questions if you approach this book with doubts or disbelief. It might open your eyes and give you deeper insights.

Is it a religion?

Buddhism is both a spiritual path and a practice that helps you to see the truth. Its core philosophy is about the path to awakening that allows one to develop wisdom, awareness, kindness, and other qualities. Is it just a philosophy?

There are many contradictions surrounding Buddhism. Some say it is a religion, while others, especially Westerners, believe that Buddhism is simply a way to inquire and contemplate the world without praising any Gods. Which one is correct?

It all depends on how you view it. There is no right or incorrect answer. If religion is all about God, and you believe religion should be about Him, then Buddhism is not a religion in Western terms. It doesn't fear or worship the supernatural. If you believe religion is not about the omnipotent divinity or blind faith but rather about looking beyond the superficial and living a life that's forgiving, and being ready to face death with serenity, then it can be called a religion.

Buddhism appeals to everyone, regardless of whether it is a religion or a philosophy or practice. This is primarily because of its simplicity. It is a way of life that teaches us a deeper, more meaningful and conscious way to live. This is something we all strive for but fail to attain. Buddhism is the way to get there. It is up to each individual to follow it.

The Birth of Buddhism

It all began with Buddha, as you may be aware. Many people mistakenly believe that Buddha is a God for Buddhists in the same way Jesus Christ is for Christians. The word Buddha, in its true essence, means "the one who is awake", clearly referring to the one who has woken to reality. Buddha is a title given to Siddhartha Gautama.

Yes, indeed, the Buddha meditating statue we have today was actually made by a real person. Siddhartha Gautama was approximately 2,600 years old, somewhere near the border between India and Nepal. Siddhartha Gautama was born as a prince who, despite all the material comforts he received, could not find fulfillment in material pleasures. Siddhartha, at 29 years of age, left his palace to pursue the true meaning of life. Although he had spent many years learning from different philosophers and teachers, it wasn't until he was 35 that he discovered true tranquility. Siddhartha discovered the true power of meditation after 6 years of practice. Siddhartha was sitting beneath a fig tree at the time. The Bodhi Tree is today a powerful symbol of Buddhism.

After he discovered that meditation can relieve stress, he began to dig deeper into the practice. He started peeling away layers of his self and tried to find the true meaning of the universe and the world. Siddhartha was known as Buddha after he found his inner equilibrium and opened his mind completely.

He wasn't a prophet or a God and certainly not speaking to God. Although he didn't have a vision of the future, he did experience enlightenment after years of practice in letting go of all things that were not truly important. Buddha began sharing his path to enlightenment and teaching others how to see the same things he saw.

Who practices it?

To become a Buddhist, you don't have to shave your hair, wear an orange robe, and go to a Tibetan monastery. Things are much simpler today than they were when Buddha began to teach the path of awakening. In the 21st Century, it is easier to become Buddhist than 25 centuries ago, when you had to be a tagalong follower of your wandering teacher to become ordained.

While you might think you need to be a monk to become a Buddhist, and to stop engaging in any activities you don't like, accepting Buddha isn't so difficult.

Nearly 10% of the world's population practices Buddhism. Most of these practitioners are ordinary people just like you and I. You will need to understand the core of Buddhism before you can make such a commitment. Then you can decide if Buddhism is the right path for you. Only then can you begin to practice Buddhism and take part in its ancient traditions.

Chapter 2: Buddhism

Let me give you a brief overview of Buddhism. Buddhism, like all other beliefs, does not believe God. What it believes in is the "self". Buddhists have all the power that other religions give God. They also give it to God.

First, I will tell you why they don't believe in God. Then, we will move to the second part. We will discuss how Buddhism can be a great way for peaceful living, what they mean by success, their values and how you can be a part.

Why don't they believe in God?

Before we proceed, please remember that every teaching of Buddhism can be interpreted according to your own intellect. Although the definitions and understandings I will give you might not be accepted by some Buddhists, I believe that the true spirit of Buddhism lies in the following understanding.

Three reasons Buddhists reject God are: Buddhists have taken their beliefs and values directly from Buddha. According to the text, Buddha discovered the power and keys to a peaceful existence when he drowned in meditation. It seemed like Buddha was only diving in his own depths, although some may argue that it was actually the idea of God that he did so. Buddhists consider every God's power to be the self's power. This means that they understand that the "self" we refer to as God is really their "self." This way you may have a better understanding of the differences between religions and sects. You should remember your old belief in God every time you use the word "self".

It is important to note that Buddhists don't believe in God (as Christians, Muslims, and Jews believe):

To erase fear

Buddhists believe that God was created in primitive times, when the world was just beginning to function. This is when humans were struggling to find their way and were uncertain of what to do. Buddhists, however, believe that this is a small reason for such a large idea to be believed by all men in the world. Let's face facts. This is a fact.

You may have felt helpless in dark times. Buddhists would seek to solve their problems by meditating and talking to themselves. One must be able to count on oneself and work hard to overcome the suffering that is causing it. He should simply understand the whole thing.

No evidence

Buddhists also reject the notion of God because there isn't any evidence to support it. While people from other religions may believe that God is feminine or masculine, God can also be called God, God is Christ and many others, none of these ideas have any evidence to prove who and what God is. Buddhists believe that there is nothing close to the idea God.

They suspend any judgments about God until evidence is presented.

Unnecessary

Third, Buddhists don't believe in God because they consider it unnecessary. This idea of God has been promoted by followers of other religions to help them explain the origins of the universe. On the other hand, Buddhists also have an idea about the origins of the world (which we'll discuss in the next chapters), and they consider the idea of God completely unnecessary. Buddhists believe science has proved the existence and origins of the universe. If this is true, why would they need to explain God? While many people believe that the idea of God is important for a balanced and successful life, there are many atheists who live a happy and fulfilled life without any need to know God. Others religions might say the same thing. This is because everyone, whether they are atheists or religious believers, has the idea of God. Accordingly to atheist beliefs, there is no difference between what the religiousists consider "everything" and what the atheists consider "nothing." However, Buddhism's true spirit is not to deny any religion but to accept whatever belief one holds. This belief can be reassured that the question about God is not a part of the list. It is better to move on and accept the beliefs the Buddhists hold to than to reject them.

These are the reasons why Buddhists don't believe in God. It is believed that God is beyond all questions and that questioning other religions and beliefs is not within the Buddhist's purview. They believe in love, harmony, and unity. They believe in the ground that unites all. This religion takes all the titles and names and gives a wider, more open, freer space to each individual to live in their own niche.

Chapter 3: The Teachings Of Buddhism

The Buddha taught many important lessons, and each deserves its own book. This chapter will not attempt to cover all aspects of each teaching. Instead, it will give an overview of some of the basics. If you're still curious, you can check out the actual sutras or vinayas (the principal texts that contain the teachings and methodology for Buddhism).

There are many fundamental concepts that make up Buddhism. These foundational concepts form the philosophy Buddhists follow. These concepts include, among others:

The Four Noble Truths

These four concepts are commonly considered the core doctrine of Buddhism. These four concepts provide the foundation for all Buddhist philosophy. These are the four noble truths:

Dukkha is often translated to mean suffering, dissatisfaction or general unhappiness.

Samudaya Sacca is a common translation of samuday as origin or source, while sacca refers to reality or truth. This refers to the true origins or causes of suffering.

Nirodha Sacca is a term that means extinction, cessation, and sacca again means reality, truth. This refers to the fact suffering (dukkha), can be stopped so that they cease to exist. This is the total and eternal elimination of suffering.

The Noble Eightfold Path: This final truth refers to the Buddha's path towards achieving Nirvana.

Below, we will discuss each of these truths in greater detail.

Dukkha

According to Buddha's teachings on suffering, it can be divided into three categories.

There are many things that will cause physical and mental suffering.

Anxiety is a way to avoid suffering. When you try to control your emotions and keep what you want, or get frustrated when you don't get what you want, this is called stress.

A general feeling of unsatisfaction that affects all forms of existence. This is because all life forms are temporary and lack an inner core or substance. It is difficult to describe, but this is a subtle concept. It is commonly understood as the suffering that is caused by holding on to the self instead of allowing yourself to be open and accepting the fact that you are one and the same with all things.

These three types of suffering are further sub-divided into dukkha, which can be further broken down into eight types.

First category:

Birth: The shock and discomfort that comes with experiencing the world for first time, or having to deal with new demands or experiences.

Old age: The discomfort and pain that comes with the natural process and progression of aging. This includes both the mental and physical aspects of the process.

Illness is the mental and physical distress that comes with being sick.

Death: This includes both the fear of your own death and the physical pain that could be caused by the process.

Second category:

You are unable to avoid situations that are difficult or unfavorable.

You may not be able to keep what your heart desires: This refers to the pain caused by holding on to something you value (e.g. a person you love, a way to live or a material possession).

It's frustrating to not be able to achieve what you want, whether you have strong feelings or you can't afford it. The anxiety and frustration that comes with not being able get what you want causes great suffering.

Third category:

All-pervasive pain: This is a subtle feeling of dissatisfaction that exists all the time in all living beings. This inward struggle, almost unconscious, to hold on to a concrete, unchanging sense or self, even though in reality nothing is permanent or unchanging.

Buddhism encourages meditation on suffering and the ways to overcome it. It has been so well categorized and described within the philosophy.

Samudaya Sacca

The second of the Four Noble Truths focuses on the origins and evolution of all forms of dukkha. Understanding the causes of suffering is essential to eliminate it from your life and reach nirvana.

According to Buddhist philosophy, suffering can be caused by cravings or indulgences (tanha), which are done out of ignorance about the nature of existence and the nature of suffering. Three main types of tanha can cause dukkha.

Kama Tanha is the search for sensory pleasures that stimulate the senses and please them. You can include beautiful objects, delightful music, tasty foods, pleasant smells, and sexual desires. These things are not necessarily forbidden, nor are they the cause of suffering. Rather, the desire for them and the conscious pursuit of sensory pleasures (rather than pursuing nirvana) are a cause of suffering-- particularly the types in the first and second categories.

Bhava Tanha is the desire to be. It is the desire to exist as an individual ego, to be stable and permanent. It can also be used to refer to the desire to be superior or dominant over others. This is the root cause for the third type of suffering.

Vibhava Tanha is the opposite of the first category. It is the desire to not be. This can be suicidal thoughts, or just the desire to be free from all the pain and experiences that the world has to offer. This can lead to suffering similar to that described in the second category.

Ignorance is the root cause of all three types of suffering. This refers both to ignorance about the literal meanings and the true implications of the Four Noble Truths. This can also be a fundamental misinterpretation of the nature and purpose of existence.

These three emotions are commonly called the three poisons. They can be summarized as: ignorance, attachment (to pleasure), or aversion (towards that which is not desirable). These three emotions (or poisons), are what you need to eliminate in order to stop suffering.

Understanding these causes will help you to identify the one that is causing you pain.

Nirodha Sacca

Nirodha Sacca, the third of Four Noble Truths is the realization that suffering can be stopped. This is more than a temporary end to suffering. It is the total cessation all dukkha so that it does not return in your life.

This is the complete release of suffering that is combined with enlightenment according Buddhist philosophy. This truth will help you see that even though it can be difficult to practice the Buddhist techniques (it requires you resist your sensory desires and allow yourself to go completely), you have good reasons to do so.

Understanding the nature and cause of suffering (Dukkha), and how it affects you (the 3 Tanhas), will help you to better understand the third truth and achieve the ultimate release from suffering.

This is the core of Buddhist philosophy. It is about achieving a state of complete peace, free from all suffering. The Noble Eightfold Path, which Buddha created to help achieve this goal will be discussed next.

The Noble Eightfold Path

The Noble Eightfold Path, which is the Buddhist method of achieving nirvana and eliminating all suffering from one's life, is the Noble Eightfold Path. You can achieve inner peace, awakening or enlightenment by following these 8 simple steps as described by Buddha.

This path aims to eradicate the "poisonous" flaws of anger, ignorance, greed. This was not a new concept even during Siddhartha Gautama's time. These same flaws were also addressed in the ascetic's own life, which he had lived before establishing The Middle Way. Siddhartha discovered that asceticism was too extreme.

The Noble Eightfold Path therefore includes those elements of asceticism that Siddhartha found helpful, but also other elements that make them more useful.

More balanced

You will see the symbol called the dharmawheel, which has eight spokes that represent each aspect of Buddhism as you continue to read.

Every aspect of the Noble Eightfold Path starts with the word "samma", which refers to ideal or right. These are the eight aspects of this path:

Samma Ditthi: The right view refers to having the right attitude or outlook towards life and the world around you. This is about understanding the reality of life. This is the first step in which practitioners learn the reasoning that will allow them to move on to the next stage. A person is considered to be right if he or she can clearly understand the law of karma (discussed further below), the three characteristics that make up existence (discussed further below) and the suffering or Dukkha (discussed previously). This understanding will clear the way to nirvana from confusion and misunderstanding. Ignorance is one of the three poisons.

Samma Sankappa: It is very important to have the right intention in Buddhism. The right thoughts and aspirations will help you to be able to focus your efforts on the Noble path and not accidentally stray from it. You should try to eliminate any bad or unsavory habits or qualities. This is the first step. This is where the first element comes in. The right intention is a strong commitment and goodwill toward others.

Samma Vava (Right Speech),: This element highlights the importance of what you say. While it is important to have the right views and the right intentions, if your speech doesn't align with these things, it is useless. The key to cultivating the right speech is to avoid abusive language, manipulation speech, lying, or idle chatter. It is making an effort to speak truthfully, the whole truth and nothing but truth. It is being polite, kind and trustworthy. You must think before you speak in order to deliver a perfect speech. You must determine if the speech you intend to deliver meets these three conditions.

It is true?

Are there any benefits?

Is it the right moment to say it?

Do not answer any of the three questions if you are unable to say no. It can be hard because we often speak casually and don't think about it. It is an integral part of the Noble Eightfold Path, and it cannot be ignored.

Samma Kammanta: Right action is just as important, if not more important than right speech. Right action refers to living a peaceful and moral life in accordance with Buddhist principles. Avoiding any act that could cause harm or be considered immoral is the key to right action. It will be much easier to achieve this goal if you have the right perspective so you can clearly determine what actions should be avoided and which ones are moral. Violent and criminal acts are the most dangerous. To avoid taking an animal's life, Buddhists are known to eat vegetarianism.

Samma Ajiva, or Right Livelihood: This element of the Noble Eightfold Path is similar to right action. It requires that you abstain from any occupation that directly or indirectly causes harm to another living thing. You should not do work that is harmful or immoral in order to support yourself. Our lives are largely spent at work, so it is crucial that our work is consistent with the Buddhist philosophy we follow. Here are five types of work that a Buddhist should not do:

Any kind of weapon can be sold or manufactured

Prostitution, slave trading and human trafficking of all kinds are prohibited.

Everything related to the meat industry, even breeding animals for slaughter.

Producing or selling alcoholic beverages.

Manufacturing or selling poisons or other toxins that are designed to cause death.

Samma Vayama (Right effort): This is essential for reaching nirvana. It is about being persistent in your efforts to cultivate each element as you travel further along your spiritual path. You must also put your efforts into the right things (which requires good intention) to ensure that your efforts are not wasted. Instead of dwelling on how hard or tiring it may be, keep your mind on the goal and work to create environments and situations that are in your favor. The four elements of right effort are:

Let go of any immoralities that you currently have.

Prevention or avoidance of immoralities that have not yet occurred in you.

Maintaining your morality.

You have not yet developed the ability to cultivate and strengthen your morality.

Samma Sati: Also called right awareness, right attention or right awareness, it refers to being alert and aware of any changes that affect the body or mind. This is about cultivating a strong focus, and an acute awareness for the moment. A Buddhist should always be present, alert, open, and present in all situations. Focusing on the future or past regrets is a waste of time and can prevent you from fully enjoying the moment. Practitioners can be more open to the present and free themselves from the burdens of the past or future worries by focusing on the present.

Samma Samadhi: Right concentration, or right meditation, is the act of clearing your mind to allow you to experience enlightenment. This meditation can be practiced using a combination breathing exercises, mantra repetitions and focusing your gaze onto a stationary object. This will strengthen the Noble Eightfold Path's seven elements. Meditation is an important tool in Buddhism. It is also widely used outside of Buddhism because it has many health benefits. The next chapter will provide more information on meditation and how to do it effectively.

Additional Terms and Definitions

These are just a few of the foundational concepts of Buddhist philosophy. As you dig deeper into the teachings, you'll also encounter some other terms and concepts. These are the most common terms you'll see:

Karma: The word karma literally translates to "action, work or deed". However, in this context it refers the idea of causality. This means that the future will be influenced by the past actions and intentions of individuals. We would normally say that "what goes around, comes around" in the West. However, Karma is much more global. Karma is closely tied to the concept of rebirth. If you do something wrong in this life, it will be carried over into your next. Karma refers to the principle that one should be good and moral to ensure future happiness.

This is the ultimate goal for every Buddhist: Nirvana. Nirvana refers to a state of total and uninterrupted peace, and oneness with all things. Nirvana literally means "blowing out", or "extinguishing". It is the point at which all suffering ceases and oneness with everything has been achieved. The point at which one reaches nirvana is when one is freed from the cycle of rebirth. According to Buddhist doctrine, Nirvana is a state of mind that continues even after one dies. The soul is then released.

These are the Three Marks of Existence. They are three common characteristics shared by all living things. To have right view, a Buddhist must consider and comprehend all three. This is one of the elements of The Noble Eightfold Path. These three characteristics are Anicca (discussed in the above), Dukkha (discussed in the below), and Anatta.

Unique: This term means "impermanence", and it refers to the Buddhist belief that all existence is constantly changing. No matter what happens, time passes without pause. However, Nirvana is a state that is beyond time, where there is no decay, change or death.

Anatta literally means "not-self" which refers to the illusion or self. The Buddha says that there is no such thing "the self" because there is no inner substance. All things are one, so any notion of "I" and "mine" is a lie. This is why it is important to constantly open yourself to the universe and to let go of the ego.

These teachings will help you to understand how to apply them in your own life. The next chapter will discuss the Buddhist techniques.

Chapter 4: How to Have the Right Action, Right Life, and Right Effort

Being able to take the right action means we are able to make positive changes in the world. Buddhists refer this as fulfilling our dharma. Dharma, which can be translated as "special purpose", is the act of actively engaging in your true calling in life. If we are pursuing our true purpose and aiming for the "right livelihood", we can have the "right actions" and "right effort" without any problems.

We are conscious of making efforts to do the things we are naturally good at when we reach our dharma. It is possible to take the right actions that will allow us to fulfill our true purpose in this life. Deepak Chopra says that it is only when we can step out of the world's petty wants that we can claim our "Evolutionary purpose".

The right kind of livelihood is essential for our evolutionary purpose. We need to make the effort to find the right job that will give us the best possible livelihood. There is a purpose to life. We just need to find it. All of us were meant to do something important. Only society's harsh constraints have made us think otherwise.

We start our lives with grandiose dreams of becoming doctors, lawyers and astronauts. When we were young, we had the right idea and dreamed big about a dharmic mission outside of ourselves. Buddhism teaches that these feelings should not be ignored. Instead, you should never stop striving for the right actions and efforts that will lead to the right livelihood that fulfills your true purpose.

When it comes to our ultimate occupation, we don't need to settle. You don't have to settle for what you do best. Just like the cheesy poster at your junior high school once said, "You can achieve anything you put your mind to." This is not just a teen pep talk. It is a reality. We can accomplish anything we put our efforts and take the necessary actions.

The right livelihood means having a job that is both rewarding and sustainable. For example, a drug dealer may make a lot of money by selling his wares at the street corner. However, he or she is inherently hurting others with their actions. This person is ignoring all three precepts. He or she puts the wrong effort into the wrong livelihood, and creates harm for others by his/her wrong actions.

It is more than just being able to make money and being successful in the worldly sense. The right livelihood is about achieving the God-given purpose (dharma), that each person has to make the world a better. It is always positive to pursue your true purpose. All of the Buddhist precepts will naturally flow smoothly if we do the things we love and put in the effort to reach our true purpose.

Chapter 5: The Eightfold Path

One of the foundations of Buddhist philosophy is The Eightfold Path. The Eightfold Path was the result of the search for spiritual direction. This is the fourth noble truth and teaches us how to end our own sufferings. Because improvement is only possible through consistent and constant practice, the Eightfold Path is more action-oriented.

Many people tend to gravitate towards extremes in order to escape suffering. Some people indulge in hedonistic pleasures to satisfy all their desires. Others seek to soothe the pain through self-mortification. Buddha states that suffering will not bring about liberation from suffering. It is not the same as the first extreme.

The Eightfold Path is a comprehensive approach that will guide anyone seeking wisdom. The first two paths focus on achieving the right mindset to reach the goal. The fourth and fifth paths focus on ethical behavior that should be followed in order to attain enlightenment. The sixth, seventh, and final path are focused on mental development that can be helpful until the end.

Keep in mind that The Eightfold Path is not an exact guide. It doesn't mean that you have to follow a specific sequence. These are interdependent principles and components that all contribute to the improvement in the follower.

The Right View

Buddha begins with the Right View, because he emphasizes the importance of understanding and vision in his journey to enlightenment. The Right View is a deep understanding and appreciation of the Four Noble Truths. Buddha does not want to see blind followers. Understanding is essential. He wants his followers to see the value of each person's journey.

The right view does not necessarily depend on intellectual ability. Meditation, insight, and a deeper understanding of the world's workings are all necessary to get there. It's a way of seeing the world that leads to right thinking and action.

2. 2. The Right Intention

The Right View is focused on understanding, but the Right Intention is focused on purpose. The right intention is not concerned with the mental aspect of our actions, but the energy that drives them. This requires a close examination of the motivations behind an act.

It is easy to let go of our desires for pleasure by having the Right View and the right Intention. This leads to harmony and oneness with all of life. It makes it easier for others to show kindness and compassion. This helps to counteract the negative emotions of hate, greed, and discontentment.

3. The Right Speech

Buddhist tradition recognizes that words have power (or lack thereof). It is clear that speech is important, especially when talking about truth and enlightenment.

Mental strength and purification are necessary to control one's tongue. Right Speech isn't as simple as it sounds. It takes wisdom to be able say the right words at the right moment. Only ethical practice and thoughtfully writing thoughts will lead to the development of Right Speech.

4. The Right Action

When seeking enlightenment, it is natural to focus on Right Actions. Buddha emphasizes the importance of abstaining actions that can cause harm to silent beings. He also advises against taking what isn't due and abstaining sexual indulgences. It requires compassion, generosity, and kindness in all relationships with other creatures. The precepts provide details about the right actions.

5. 5. The Right Lifestyle

Buddha understands the importance work plays in achieving enlightenment. His disciples are taught to choose a wise occupation and not to do any work that could cause harm. Weaponry, butchery and prostitution are just a few examples of trades that should be avoided. Any form of livelihood that encourages hypocrisy and trickery should also be avoided.

6. The Right Effort

Without the Right Effort, nothing will have any meaning. It would be impossible to achieve anything and all things will be an act or will. It would be difficult for people to direct their efforts in the right direction without the right mental energy. It's easy to become lazy. It's easy to get misguided. The right effort can transform your life and help you understand the world better.

7. The Right Mindfulness

The ability to see clearly is called Right Mindfulness. It is a cognitive skill that starts with a thought or perception and moves to conceptualization. Right Mindfulness refers to being more aware of the direction of your own thoughts. It reminds us that we have control over our own thoughts. His followers are encouraged to be more contemplative by Buddha. To be able to control one's own thoughts, one must make thinking more conscious.

8. The Right Concentration

Right concentration is when one's mind is unifying. Concentration is the unidirectional mind.

Are you one of those people who has ever felt disorganized and confused? When your ideas are all in one place, it's difficult to be productive. You'll find yourself jumping from one task to the next without ever achieving anything concrete.

Concentration is the ability to focus all of your mental faculties on one object and not be distracted by external forces. Although it takes some effort to focus on one thing for long periods of time, it will help you harness all your energy and direct it. Your meditative experiences will eventually become more intense as you gain control over your thoughts. Meditation is a great way to improve your concentration.

Chapter 6: Walking Towards awakening: Learning The Path

The Fourth Noble Truth teaches us that there is a way, a way to end sufferings or dukkha. This is the "how" while the first three noble Truths serve as the "what's". As we've already said, there is much more to Buddhism than just the discussion of the Four Noble Truths. However, these serve as the starting points for deeper and more detailed discourses about Buddhism.

What is the Eightfold Path and How Does It Work?

The fourth noble truth describes a path or area of practice that reveals to someone what is ideal or right. It is not a directive telling a person what to do, or a commandment. It is the path, as Buddhist essence understands it, that teaches a person how to practice every aspect of the path. It encompasses all aspects of one's life. The path is represented as the spokes on a wheel. The wheel will turn once you know which spoke is the first or the eighth. All spokes make the wheel stronger and more efficient. A wobbly wheel may be caused by a lack of importance or getting rid of a spoke. This is just as when you are practicing the path. Uneven concentration is not possible because each practice area is crucial in the realization of the cessation or awakening of dukkha.

To practice Buddhism, one must be proficient in three areas. These areas are Wisdom, Ethical Conduct, and Mental discipline.

The following are the components of the Wisdom Path:

* The Right View or Right Understanding, as some literature might suggest. This insight reveals the first three noble truths, the nature and origin of dukkha as well as the extinction of the dukkha.

* Right Intention, Right Thought, or Right Aspiration refers to the intention to attain enlightenment. It is free from any attachment to cravings or desires. One could argue that there is no goal to become or not become, which separates a person from other people.

The Ethical Path includes the following:

* Harmony-promoting speech or right speech Truthful speech is not influenced by malice. This does not mean that you should say "nice" things if there is a need.

* Compassion is the foundation of ethical action. You can do something without attachment or selfishness.

* Right Living is a means of earning a living that does not compromise the happiness and well-being of others. It's earning without causing harm to anyone.

These are the components of The Mental Discipline Path:

* Right effort, or Right Diligence, is the ability to develop healthy qualities in yourself and release unwholesome traits.

* Right mindfulness, or awareness of the moment through the use of the whole body;

* Right concentration is most closely linked to meditation. This involves focusing on your mental faculties and practicing the four dhyanas, or four states of mind.

As we have said, practicing the various areas of the path will enable an individual to embrace the Way of the Buddha. Legend has it that Prince Siddharta was mixed up at first when he experienced enlightenment. He didn't want to share this knowledge with others. He believes that he cannot teach something so profound that words and human experience are not able to adequately explain it. However, the Buddha encouraged him to share what was learned. He was convinced. He found no other way to express himself. So he began to share his experiences and show others how it works. This is the foundation for the fourth noble truth. This is the Path.

Next chapter will be about meditation in Buddhist terms. The next chapter will discuss how meditation can lead to inner peace and enlightenment.

Chapter 7: The Belief Systems

It doesn't take a Buddhist practice to believe in the same things that Buddhists believe. Many Buddhist principles are not known to ordinary people. It doesn't matter how many Buddhism aspects throw you off-guard, it is important to look into other Buddhist interests. It's possible to change your whole week, or even your entire life with one belief.

Anatma is a Buddhist belief that says one being is always changing. This is a crucial lesson to learn. It is important to have a positive self-image. This will help you to be more confident in your actions. This belief holds that nothing is fixed and that we can shape our lives to what we want.

Anatma also shares two other beliefs, Dukkha (and Anitya). These two beliefs help us understand that the world and its events are not permanent. All you need to prevail over the negative events in your life is patience and time. You have the patience and time to get even further if you've come this far. These beliefs can be easily applied to our daily lives. Accepting change can help you see the bigger picture and open up to new opportunities.

If you dig deeper into Buddhism beliefs, the Five Precepts of Buddhism will be revealed. You will quickly see that these precepts are a simpler way to live. These rules are not necessarily religious commandments. You must not lie, steal, use drugs, alcohol or sex to kill. Buddhism is a right way to live. To achieve that, you need to eliminate all negative factors that might interfere with the process of awakening. These guidelines are not all that we should expect. There are five more. These include refusing to accept gold or silver, avoiding perfume and high-seat use, and many other things.

The Four Noble Truths are one of the most popular belief systems in Buddhism. These beliefs focus on your struggles and how they can be reduced. This means that you can come to terms with your surroundings and reality. The Noble Eightfold Path will help you to find out exactly what The Noble Eightfold Path has to offer you. This path will teach you how to manage everyday tasks like speech, livelihood and mindfulness. This obstacle can be hard to overcome due to the constant thoughts of your stress. It is possible with the right help.

Although the Noble Eightfold Path has been called many things and given different definitions, it serves one purpose. Its sole purpose is to bring happiness, enlightenment and joy into the lives of those who choose to follow it. This process helps you to overcome all the difficulties that can arise, as well as your demons. The Noble Eightfold Path and the Four Noble Truths are two ways to help you live a positive, healthy life. These steps can help you achieve the life and personality that you have always wanted.

Buddhism often refers to reincarnation. Buddhists believe that you will reincarnate after your death. Many people may experience this cycle multiple times. Karma, wisdom, and compassion are all other beliefs. You will discover that Buddhism is a message of happiness as you learn more about it. These beliefs are important in your quest for happiness. Your actions must be viewed against the backdrop of others. Karma can be described as an award system. Buddhists believe that a punishment should be applied to those who do a wrong deed. It would be the reverse when a good deed is done.

These beliefs can have positive effects on your life. However, you should approach each one with caution as they may open up new feelings that you didn't know existed. You will get through it all and be happier in the end. These insights were only shared by the Buddha to aid his followers. You must believe that you are strong enough to overcome any obstacle. Even though the Buddha is no more with us, many of his beliefs and teachings have remained a lasting impression on people.

Chapter 8: The Twins Known As Enlightenment and Darkness

Buddhism doesn't believe in heaven or hell outside of ourselves. Rather, Buddhism believes heaven and hell only exist in our minds and hearts. Heaven and hell are only as real as the quality of our thoughts, and the depth of compassion we have. This is what creates heaven and hell, and how we perceive the world around us from moment to moment. Hell is made from the illusions we create in our minds and belief in their validity.

Each person has an enlightened part of themselves. The qualities of wisdom, compassion and courage are all part of an enlightened nature. All of life has these qualities. Anything that hinders us from experiencing our inner light is a part of our darkness. Both the enlightened as well as dark sides of ourselves are always present. Our ability to transcend darkness leads us to our enlightenment. In contrast, our inability to transcend and detect our darkness makes it more powerful, subordinating our ability to attain enlightenment. Buddhism's purpose is to transcend our darkness.

Mindfulness or Presence

Greg gets up every morning to get ready for work. He is planning his day even before he gets out of bed. He considers what he must do to get to work. Greg recalls the intimate conversation he had the other day with his girlfriend while he takes a shower. He also considers the fact that he still has to choose a gift for his parents' anniversary. Greg drives to work in his car, thinking about how much he would love to camp. Greg arrives at work and spends the day thinking about his next meeting, returning phone calls, and making the right decisions to increase the profitability of his department. Greg ends the day by sitting down to watch a movie. He is enjoying the movie but his mind drifts off occasionally as he considers the issues that concern him. These thoughts continue to haunt him until he goes to bed. He then stops thinking about them when he falls asleep.

Greg is representative of the vast majority, as he lives his entire life using the time machine called thought. The past (which is called memory) and the future (which are called anticipation) make up the majority of our thoughts. These two thoughts consume the majority of our lives, at the expense or mindfulness of being present and mindful. We cannot experience the present if we focus on the future or the past. Buddhists see time as an illusion that is created by the mind. We can only experience the present moment and memory. What is the present, or the moment now? Awareness is the only constant. Awareness is the only constant. Thoughts and perceptions, feelings, sensations, and experiences change constantly; however awareness is constant. You are the moment. Your awareness is your presence.

Exercise

Choose a comfortable place. You can choose to be indoors or outside. Relax and sit down. Take a few minutes to simply look around. Pay attention to what you feel within yourself. Do not evaluate, analyze, or judge what you see. It is your job to observe. You can observe it for longer than 10 minutes if you wish. This can be repeated each day to increase your observation time. Relaxation is key when doing this exercise. This exercise cannot be done wrong. Even if you make a judgement, let yourself be open to experiencing this without judgment.

Self-identification with the Body and Mind

Are your thoughts in control? Are you aware about the sensations in your body? Are you aware about your perceptions? Are you aware of the health and well-being of your body? Are you aware of your body? You cannot be these things if you are not aware of them. Nevertheless, the majority of us base our identity on our bodies and minds. Worry can permeate our whole being if we are anxious. Our being is affected by sadness when we feel sad. When we feel in love, this is what we experience. We identify with our bodies and minds, so we perceive ourselves as separate. This is why this eBook will not confuse your senses of self. You cannot be anything other than your mind and body because you are a part of them. However, this illusion is also possible. Deep sleep is a state of complete consciousness that leaves you without any sense of self or experience. Deep sleep is pure consciousness. This is unlike REM sleep where you can experience dreams. Your essential being, as I mentioned earlier, is awareness.

Exercise

You should find a comfortable and quiet spot to rest. You can either sit on the ground or in a chair.

Relax by closing your eyes. Focus on your breath when you inhale. Observe the sensations your breath makes as it leaves your body. Relax and breathe naturally. It is vital that you don't exert any effort during meditation. You can also observe the rise and fall of your abdomen by following your breath.

You will feel thoughts, sensations, perceptions and thoughts as you breathe. They will all have different qualities. Some may be pleasant, while others might be unpleasant or even scary. Do not try to control, change or analyze them. You cannot control, modify, or analyze them. Be like a scientist, who is only interested in observing them.

Be aware of the mental functions you are observing as you observe them. You are the one who is watching thought, sensation, perception, and other mental functions. Find the one doing the observing. Remember that not everything you can see with your eyes can be the one doing the observing. It is also being observed.

Chapter 9: Happiness Doesn't Depend on What You Have or Who You Are. It All Depends on What You Think" - Buddha

Young hearts might struggle to grasp the truth that old age can bring out: who you are, what achievements you make, or what possessions you own, don't really matter. What matters is how you see the world and the people you have helped, directly or indirectly. Your possession will die, so no one cares. It doesn't matter what kind of personality you might present, because it will all be forgotten.

Too many people try to be someone they're not. Only to find out later that it was a mistake and a way to impress others who care more about themselves than the rest. You are enough inside. You just need to bring out that side. Do not try to hide your true self with layers of superficial personality to please others or avoid rejection. You can be quiet and a deep thinker if you are naturally quiet. You can be a natural entertainer or someone who enjoys being in the centre of attention. Accept your unique personality traits, which are the ones you were born with and not those you have cultivated to please others or avoid rejection. This will allow you to be comfortable in a world that often sees superficial traits take the spotlight. You will be happier if you live your authentic self. There is nothing worse than being compared to others for what you aren't, or having other people around you who want your possessions.

Buddha said, "Do not dwell on the past, don't dream about the future, focus your attention on the present moment."

Some people are stuck in the past while others are stuck in the future. Only a few can experience the true beauty and joy of life. A way of living that does not involve past suffering but builds a better future. This is the way to live. This is the moment you have now, and it's the only time in your life. All of your life's experiences, joy and pain, were made in the present moment. This may seem simple at first, but simplicity is the home for love and providence.

Why is it important to live in the moment? You can't live in this moment if you think about the future or the past. This is something most people don't realize. It's the state of being unaware that can be most dangerous. People keep replaying past events and thinking about past pain, which can lead to a mental breakdown. But what about the other side? One person fails to embrace the moment and instead looks ahead, where doom, gloom, and things that could go wrong are all around.

This is what you get when you are able to live in the future or past on a regular basis. The majority of people on earth won't allow themselves to live in the present moment fully. This is because it can be too difficult to stop thinking about the future or past. They are correct, unfortunately. The human mind is wired to do this. The mind bounces back and forth between the past and the future, seldom focusing on the present moment. This way of living, in the past and future, is our primal side. It feels the need to constantly be thinking, alert, and on top of possible dangers. In today's world, acting on primal instincts is not a good idea.

The mind isn't perfect. It still struggles to adapt to our rapid evolution as an species. Not too long ago, we lived in twenty-person tribes. It's safe for us to say that we are still primal-bound, considering the millions of years ago that skeletons were discovered.

You have to be against your instincts if you want happiness and to achieve great things. You must resist your natural instinct to eat junk food, and instead stay home and do nothing if you want to become fit. You must be a entrepreneur if you want success. Your natural instincts will tell you to avoid making mistakes and to stay within your comfort zone. But if you want your business to thrive, you have to accept discomfort and make lots of mistakes.

It's the same as living in the moment. It is going against your self-behavior. Although it may feel uncomfortable initially, the long-term benefits will be priceless. You will see the color of your life again. The best part is that you won't be trapped in the past or the future, replaying hurtful memories or anticipating gloomy outcomes, which only poisons this moment.

If you find yourself thinking about the past or the future, don't beat yourself up. Remember that you are only human. Your brain will naturally gravitate towards the past or future and avoid the present moment. You have to remind yourself that the only way to live in the moment, where all things happen, is to do so. You don't have to live in the moment all the time. This can be difficult. Instead, you can use your conscious mind and immerse yourself in it from time to time. It will get easier if you continue doing it, and you will soon start to reap the rewards.

It is important to think about it rationally. Is it wise not to dwell on past hurt that isn't affecting you right now? It is possible to choose to live differently and to think differently now.

"No one saves you but yourself." No one can save us. "We must all walk the path." - Buddha

Nobody is going to knock on your door and say, "I want to change your life." Let me help change your life. No friend, family member, or work colleague can do that. Why? Because each person is on their own path in life.

Your life is your fault if it is chaotic. All the small decisions you have made along the journey are what have brought you to where you are today. It could be an indication that you aren't taking 100% responsibility for your life if someone tells you you are responsible for it. Here's the key: Don't get mad, embrace it. 100% responsibility means you are responsible for the problems in your life. If you're the problem, then you can fix it 100%. It might be difficult to make changes if others are at fault, such as your family, friends, or government.

Let's face facts. You will die long before any of these things can change.

Buddha: "Three things cannot remain long hidden: The sun, the moon and the truth."

You can lie to your family, friends and co-workers but truth will always surface. And you will be the one who suffers the most. You know deep down the truth about everything. You only need to ask yourself the question. Your gut will usually give you the answer right away, either in your stomach or later as inspiration. If you are unsure about something, no matter how important it is, ask yourself if this is where you should be and watch your body react. Don't think about thoughts in your head.

Feel the sensation in your gut. Is it sinking? Is it a sinking feeling?

A single candle can light thousands of candles, so the life span of each candle is not affected. Sharing happiness does not decrease its value." - Buddha

You have more power over others than you realize. Don't think you are a pawn in the world that doesn't care. One person can inspire hope and faith in millions of people by shining light on the darkness in a world that is dark. You might think that sharing your knowledge with others would reduce your ability to give and increase your energy, but this is not true. You actually gain more love and happiness when you share your experiences with others. You will gain more if you share your knowledge with others. This is not a new concept. Too many people don't realize this power. The opposite is true, too. You will get more from others if you do not take enough. This is a lie. You can try it. Keep going and you'll feel the sinking feeling in your gut, and an increasing sense of emptyness. Keep giving and you will feel a sense of aliveness inside.

Chapter 10: Mindfulness

If you imagine a Buddhist monk sitting high on a hill in Tibet, you might also feel the inner peace the monk is feeling. He is a symbol of inner joy. He doesn't sit still and think of nothing. Meditation has a purpose. One monk might be striving to achieve self-fulfillment. He may meditate or use mindfulness.

This step requires that you sit straight with your back straight. However, you must also be breathing correctly - in through your nostrils. For a second, hold the breath and then exhale. When you breathe correctly, there is a pivoting motion in the upper abdomen. Continue to breathe in this manner until you achieve that motion. Next, pay attention to everything around you at this moment. It is important. People waste precious moments in their lives worrying about the future or thinking back. Mindfulness is being present in the moment. When asked by the Dalai Lama about his thoughts on modern man's approach towards life, he said something. It is important to remember its significance as it is crucial for mindfulness.

"Man surprised me the most about humanity. Because he is willing to sacrifice his health for the sake of making money.

He then sacrifices his health to recover it. He then sacrifices his health to recover it.

He is extremely insightful. It is easy to spend so much time dwelling on past failures or future worries that you aren't actually living in this moment. As you sit down to practice mindfulness, pay attention to your surroundings. Only pay attention to what you feel and see. You were given your senses for a special purpose. That purpose is to be able to appreciate everything happening in your daily life. You can smell the air, feel the atmosphere, and hear the sounds. If your thoughts drift to other things, acknowledge it and then dismiss it. Recognize what you are doing. But, it is equally important to know the difference between being MINDFUL or simply thinking about other matters.

Mindful eating

You can smell and taste the aroma of your food if you are attentive. Hold a cup of coffee, or any other hot beverage, to your nose and enjoy the full aroma. Next, hold the cup to your lips and let the liquid drip into your mouth. Allow it to sit for a while, then taste it and then swallow it. Enjoy the warmth of the beverage. Enjoy it with all your senses

You serve multiple purposes by doing the same thing while you eat. Another purpose is to eat slower, which will be a great benefit for your digestive system. Although you may not think of it this way, your stomach is the largest organ in your body. If you're stressed or emotionally upset, your stomach will suffer. Take the time to taste the textures and texture of every food you eat. Make sure you chew the food well for easy digestion. Take your time and enjoy your food.

Mindfulness in relationships

You will be more compassionate if you're mindful of the needs of others. While you love yourself, you know that caring for others is sometimes necessary. While you can't avoid taking responsibility for the relationships you have, you do see the benefits of friendships and don't allow your friends to doubt your honesty by criticizing someone. Mindfulness is not only about being there for your friends, but also about giving and receiving in a relationship. And it's all about learning to give and take without cost. To put it another way, when you give, don't attach a price tag to your gift or expect something in return. Expectations can make it difficult to give. STEP 2 is mindfulness. This guide will help you to move from the past into the present. You should practice it every day until you feel comfortable with how it responds to the present moment. If you fail, don't get mad at yourself. It is impossible to change the habits that you have developed over the course of your life.

Chapter 11: The beliefs that underlie Buddhism

Buddha believed in certain things and passed them on to his followers. These beliefs are passed on to every generation. Buddha believed that people should live a happier life. They will feel less stressed and pressured, and they won't burn out. He believes that people should still be open to consideration for other living things.

These beliefs are a bit more complex than I have previously discussed. You can then decide if they are true for you. The best way to fully understand Buddhism is to get rid of any preconceived notions or misconceptions and to just feel its presence.

FOUR NOBLE TRUTHS IN BUDDHISM

These are the beliefs he taught in his first sermon. This section is Buddhism 101. It contains the fundamental realities we must know.

SUFFERING IN THE WEALTH -- It is impossible to predict what the future holds. You will have times in your life where everything goes well, but then suddenly there are some unfortunate events. This is only one of the four noble truths in Buddhism.

There is always a reason behind your suffering -- What do you do when you feel sad? You might pretend you're not. We are prone to believe that we feel something other than what we really feel. We crave for something we can't have. This is where the suffering, or frustrations in modern terms, comes in. Our sufferings are caused by our inability to obtain something. To escape reality, we must connect to our past and future.

YOU CAN END YOUR SUFFERINGS. Every failure is an opportunity to succeed the next time. We tend to give in when we fail or do something wrong. Redefining yourself can help us end our sufferings.

END ALL SUFFERINGS -- This fourth noble truth of Buddhism is called "End all sufferings". The second and third noble truths are so compelling that we think they are telling us why we are suffering. The third is so convincing that we believe we can end it all and the last one will help us.

After we have fully understood the Four Noble Truths, it is time to learn about the Eightfold Path. This is how you can find the path to eternal happiness and peace of mind.

EIGHTFOLD PATH

The Eightfold Path is similar to The Ten Commandments. It is better to learn than unlearn. This involves changing old habits and traits. Learn to let go of old habits and learn the truth. This Eightfold Path can help us achieve pure happiness, especially in today's world of stress, pressure, and suffering. It is time to make a difference. Let's learn the Eightfold Path of Buddhism.

Right Understanding

It is not possible to continue to live in complacency and allow life to blind us. You need to confront your suffering and find the solution. It is important to eliminate obstacles and hindrances that prevent you from fully understanding the problem.

CLEAN INTENTION

It is possible to avoid suffering by being mindful of what we do, how we behave, and what our intentions are. To be able to behave correctly with the right actions, we must have a clear intention.

PROPER BEHAVIOR

This will result in more energy and more thinking, which will make it harder for your brain to decide whether what you are doing is right or wrong. It must always show compassion and kindness to others, not hurt them. Helping others to alleviate their stress and pain is better than putting it on them. Be mindful of what you do. It must be a positive and clear message to everyone. This will allow us to do the right thing without worrying about making mistakes or causing harm to others.

PROPER WORDS TO TALK

Use profanity sparingly, don't lie and avoid saying anything negative when you speak. Don't confuse your listener by saying anything. Words can be dangerous. They have the potential of causing more harm than a sword. People talk a lot these days, and they often speak without thinking. If a word is misused, it can lead to misinterpretation. Communications should be clear, honest, meaningful, clean, and free from any harm.

PROPER ATTITUDE TO LIVE

This section focuses on how you interact with others while working. You might find coworkers at work who don't care about how others feel about their speech, actions, and language. It is important to visualize everything and decide if this is the life you want.

PUT IT INTO ACTIONS, GET MORE EFFORT

If you can't put the Eightfold Path or beliefs of Buddha into practice, what is the point? All of it will be pointless. It is important to be mindful of the places where our efforts are being directed each day.

BE MINDFUL

It's more than just being aware or paying attention to all things. People tend to dwell on the past, no matter how terrible it was. Buddhism teaches you how to be mindful and cautious to get rid of any grudges from the past.

MEDITATE

Focus on the things you desire to achieve. Allow yourself to let go of suffering. Concentration will improve your ability to concentrate and help you relax. To be successful at meditation, you will need energy. Meditation properly will bring you peace of mind and endless hope. It will also give you the power to do good for others and yourself.

The Eightfold Path, which is described here, will lead you to the enlightenment you seek. You will feel like you have been reborn. Everything will be new again.

FIVE PRECEPTIONS

First, the Buddhist practice requires that you observe the five precepts. These are simple obligations that Buddhists and others can observe. These Five Precepts prohibit killing, stealing and false speech as well as sexual misconduct and drug use. These Precepts are to be complied with by citizens of all nations. It's easy to grasp since these are the same rules each of us follows.

These Five Precepts have multiple purposes to help us understand the world and achieve pure happiness and enlightenment. It will allow us to discern good from bad. To distinguish between good and evil, we must first motivate our actions, then look at the consequences and effects of those actions, and finally, see how they affect the people around us. This will allow you to fully reveal your passion. To increase your mental and emotional positivity, be more compassionate, love and share good wisdom. The first precept is to not kill. This precept is founded on the principles of humanity, goodwill, and respect for life and all living creatures in this world. Modern law makes killing an offense and can be punished.

The second precept, Do not Steal, refers to cultivating generosity. This helps one to let go of attachment to being selfish and encourages cooperation with the community.

False speech is when we speak to someone with a lack of kindness or honesty. This refers to our words. Words can easily cause hurt feelings. It can cut deeper than the knife, and leave scars we often recognize as hatred. It causes suffering and makes us feel bad about one another. Do not lie or give false information. This will help you maintain your credibility, honor, integrity, and trustworthiness. Buddha once stated, "There are very few evil acts that a liar can commit."

Sexual misconduct--Buddhism prohibits sexual misconduct and any other forms of sexual abuse. This is a reminder to married couples to be respectful of their spouses and to exercise self-restraint. We also prohibit sexual misconduct in modern times. It will harm your morality and your soul. It is very sad to see the number of cases and issues involving sexual misconduct. They could have saved their souls if they had practiced the Five Precepts of Buddhism.

Use no drugs or intoxicants. This applies to developing our senses of responsibility. We can suffer from many negative effects if we take drugs. It can cause harm to our bodies and even death. You may make mistakes and commit crimes to get a drink of this intoxicant. These unfortunate events can have a devastating effect on many people's lives. It would be a good idea to prevent them. Drugs can cause death, injuries, and crime, which can have negative consequences for our spirituality.

It will also be too obvious.

These Five Precepts of Buddhism are applicable to every day life. It is not that different from what is in our law. It doesn't take long to remember all this information. We just need to know it by heart. This will encourage a sense of responsibility and self-reliance as well as credibility and respect, which are all important aspects of Buddhism's morality. Even though we might make mistakes, they don't have to be repeated. We can learn from them and improve next time. Even though we live a modern lifestyle, it doesn't mean we don't need to be mindful of the value of life. It is still important to do so. There is only one life, and there will not be another except the one we have now. We must ensure that we make the most of our lives. Like what others say, "There will come a time when your life flashes right in front of your eyes." It's worth the effort.

Chapter 12: How the Impermanent Causes Us Pain and How to Avoid It

Our modern world is too dependent on temporary things. This is the biggest problem. We envy people who have more stuff, better cars, vacations, new homes, and other luxuries. Although we may try to make a difference in our happiness by spending our time on these things, it only makes us more miserable and puts us in debt.

We don't need to focus our energy on the good anymore. We no longer focus on the good, the friends, or the kind words. Instead, we are focusing on ourselves and the energy we send out to the world. It's all about status symbols, having more stuff, more money and more fame. Can't we see the problem?

Instead of focusing on the permanent things in our lives, the things that make us happy and connected, instead we focus our energy on the temporary. We are creating a need that will never go away, and a dissatisfaction in our lives if we place too much emphasis on these things.

We can begin to make changes in our behavior when we notice that others have the stuff we don't. It's easy to think about how the person who is getting a new car doesn't deserve it or how rude they are. These people may cause us to change how we treat them. Sometimes, this behavior can extend to both those who are more fortunate than us and those who may be less fortunate than us. In the hope of feeling better, we may feel envy and say negative things about them. This is a very inefficient way to make yourself feel better.

We are ultimately making ourselves miserable. All the bad energy and all the effort we put into making things more permanent are just creating karma that makes us miserable. People don't make us feel better if we have certain thoughts. Saying things that hurt or are mean to another person doesn't make us feel better. We don't feel better if we are jealous or angry because someone else has something we don't.

All this makes us feel miserable. These are the Buddhist teachings that can help us through all of this. They know that both our human nature and material objects can cause us to feel this way. This gives them a way out to help us break the cycle and feel better. Although it will be difficult work and the teachings were from years ago, there is no better time than the present to learn these lessons.

We have now learned from the Buddhist teachings, that true happiness is the path that will help us feel happy and live the best possible life. After realizing they are not the things that influence us too much, we must let go of our cravings. These cravings hold us back and make us feel lonely and miserable. We can live without the excesses and only consume what is necessary. This will allow us to save so much time and energy that we couldn't even imagine.

We also need to examine how we act towards others. It will not make us feel good if we use so much of our energy to make others feel bad. This can be with our thoughts, actions, and words. This is negative energy or karma being sent out and it is bringing it back to us. We may not be able to help the feelings of another person, but it will come back and harm us even more.

We can make a difference in how we behave towards others. This is how we will be able get so much more out of life. You will feel better if you have a positive attitude towards others. Although it may take some time, the results are positive for everyone.

It is easy to become caught up in the world of material things. They promise temporary happiness, but often make us feel worse. We need to be able see the truth, and to go through all of this, in order to find the permanent items that will make us happy and fulfilled people and ensure our karma is on the right track. It doesn't take a Buddhist to understand the tenets of Buddhism and how they relate to your life.

Chapter 13: The Eight Fold Path To True Happiness

You can view the 8-fold path from a 3 point perspective. It is divided into three stages. These three stages form the foundation upon which learning, practice, and cultivation of Buddhism are anchored. These are the stages

*Morality

*Concentration

*Wisdom

Thinking, speaking and acting are the driving forces behind values

Morality

You can further divide morality into five stages. These stages are intended to help you understand Zen practice. Morality is characterized by skillful understanding, skillful thought, skillful speech and skilled livelihood.

Concentration

This requires skillful effort, skilled mindfulness, and skillful focus. These are the final steps in the eight-step process to becoming enlightened.

Let's take a closer look at each stage. To be able to guide your mind on the right course, you need to understand the nature of life. You can think the right way by understanding that temptations and desires are part of your nature. Focus your attention on spiritual growth and not material pleasures. Ever heard of someone who said, "I'm satisfied enough"? I have yet to meet someone like this in the material world. Most rich people will do whatever it takes to make the next big win. This pursuit is futile and endless. This is a way to never be satisfied.

Buddha discovered the truth of speech in 2500 B.C. This truth was as true back then as it is today. It encourages you to speak the right words to others and yourself. It is impossible to overstate the power of the tongue. You act from your speech. You are more likely to behave badly if you speak poorly to others and say hurtful things verbally and by heart. If you speak well, show compassion, and are sensitive to others and yourself, you'll be able to do the right things and build others. You will never be influenced by outside factors to make you happy. This is how you can achieve true happiness. Only act with compassion and concern for others and yourself. Your heart is full of love. Love is the source of joy and happiness. It's true, lasting happiness.

The eightfold path emphasizes the importance of earning a living in a responsible manner. It is important to ensure that others are not hurt by your efforts to survive. You will live with peace of mind and a clear conscience. You won't live with guilt or fear from harm.

Concentration requires that you put in the effort to get what you want. It follows the natural principle action and response. You will achieve the desired results if you put in the effort and are focused on specific goals.

Concentration is only possible when you are mindful. Meditation allows you to focus your attention on the present and opens your eyes to the hidden treasures that lead to true happiness. It is possible to find a peace and joy that cannot be found by pursuing worldly pursuits. Mindfulness is all about concentration. You can focus your attention on your breathing and the meaning of such actions for you and others. This will help you get rid of the useless thoughts that clutter your mind and stop it from reaching its true potential to enjoy the gift of existence.

We will now discuss Zazen, which is an important practice in Zen Buddhism. It can also help you find inner peace and happiness.

Zazen

As we mentioned, Zazen is the meditation technique that Zen Buddhism was founded upon. Mindfulness is the main ingredient that drives Zazen. Zazen can thus be described as the heart of Zen practice. Zazen is the core of Zen practice. Zen is the practice of realizing, consciousness, and applying it. Zazen is the foundation of Zen practice and application. Let's take a look at some Zazen positions that you can do at home, in order to help you relax and embrace mindfulness.

Postures and Zazen Poses

Zazen practice is all about comfort. You can meditate longer if you are comfortable. You are not comfortable if you don't have a place that supports your weight well.

It is important to realize that your body must support your weight. For Zazen, the upright lotus position is best. This position allows the body to transfer weight downwards to cushion. To allow breathing, the ribcage can easily move. Relax your shoulders and arms. Here are some possible positions you could adopt.

Full lotus: Place your right foot on your left thigh, as high as you can, and sit down. Place your left foot on the right side of the thigh.

Half Lotus: Place your left foot on the right side of the thigh, and then move your right foot under the left.

Burmese position: Stand with one foot in front and the other on the pad.

Seiza position with bench: You will need to kneel while your rear side is supported from a bench. Your legs should be folded under the bench.

Seiza with cushion: This is the zafu (cushion), which provides primary support for your weight.

Sitting on a chair: Lean forward and place your back against the chair's backrest. To maintain an upright posture, you can use a cushion or pad if the backrest is inclined backwards.

Hand position. Madra, a Buddhist term for hand position, is also known as Madra.

The left hand of a right-handed person is placed in the right, so that the thumb tips touch lightly.

For a left-handed individual, reverse the process.

Zazen in actioin

These are the steps involved in Zazen practice:

-Sit in the most comfortable position

Stop moving and relax.

Relax your feet, trunk, arms, and head.

-Keep your spine straight in the traditional lotus position

Let your ego fly out of your system

Listen to your body. Your breathing, your body relaxing, and think only about you.

You should wear loose fitting clothes and sit correctly in order to achieve the best results.

Chapter 14: The Road to Victory

Buddhism is a simple, liberal religion. It's a path of spiritual growth and practice that can help practitioners gain insight into the real and practical nature reality. Meditation is a Buddhist practice that helps to develop kindness, wisdom, awareness. People who are seeking "Buddhahood," or full enlightenment, can benefit from the practical knowledge that Buddhists have accumulated over thousands of years. A person who is enlightened can see the truth of reality, untampered and unaltered, and live in accordance with it. This is the ultimate goal of the Buddhist spiritual life: to end suffering for those who adopt it.

The fundamental principles of Buddhist teachings are simple and practical. The following are the basic principles of Buddhism:

There is no permanent fix.

Every action has a result.

It is possible to make changes.

Buddhism is open to all people, regardless of nationality, race or gender. It offers practical ways to help people change and live lives that are fully responsible.

You may feel overwhelmed or confused if you are new to Buddhism. These questions and answers are interactive and easy-to-understand.

What is Buddhism?

Buddhism is both a religion, and a way to live. This spiritual path is followed by approximately 300 million people worldwide. The word "Buddhism", which literally means "to awaken", is derived from the word "Buddhi". Buddhism is a very ancient religion. It dates back approximately 2,500 years to Siddhartha Gautama's awakening at 35.

Buddhism is about the quest for enlightenment. It shares very few similarities with Western religions. There are no deities or sins. There is no way to save yourself. To achieve an awakened condition and help others, there is nothing Buddhists can do.

Is Buddhism a religion or not?

Buddhism is much more than a religion for many people. It is a way of living or a philosophy of living. Because philosophy is the love of wisdom, it's sometimes called a philosophy. This sums up the Buddhist path to self-enlightenment:

Pay attention to your thoughts and actions.

Develop understanding and wisdom

Live a morally upright life

What can Buddhism do for me?

Buddhism is a religion which satisfactorily explains life's purpose. It highlights the injustice and inequality that are widespread in the world. It provides a way to live that will eventually lead you into true happiness. This is something that no normal person can experience.

Enlightenment can be achieved on both small and large scales. Buddhism teaches you to accept the world as it is and to let go of your emotions. Buddhism may be right for you if you feel lost in the world and its workings. There are endless opportunities to grow and learn within yourself. Buddhism can help you understand what is going on internally and externally. It is difficult to feel anger and sadness when you surrender to Buddhist beliefs.

Why is Buddhism so popular?

There are many reasons why Buddhism is popular in the west. First, Buddhism is a religion that seems to have solutions for many of the problems in modern materialistic societies. If you're interested in the conventional human mind, it also provides a deep understanding that not even the most prominent psychologists around the globe have been able to grasp. These knowledge and depth of understanding have been found to be both extremely effective and highly advanced.

Many people find Buddhism easy to relate to because it doesn't have any strict commands. Buddhism doesn't recognize sin, and it doesn't require anyone to worship a god to be saved. Buddhism is a self-sustaining lifestyle. Each individual's ability to sustain themselves is the key. Buddhists have the freedom to go as deep or as shallow as they wish. While some chant all day, others use the practice to help them live a happy and fulfilled life. Buddhism, like all other things, can be customized and tailored to the individual. It allows practitioners to seek their happiness and not depend on others' compliance.

Who was the Buddha?

Siddhartha Gautama (also known as "Buddha") was born to a Lumbini royal family in 563 BC. Siddhartha realized at the age of 29 that wealth and luxury were not enough to guarantee happiness and success in life. To find the secret to happiness, Siddhartha began to study the religious teachings of his day. He finally found the "middle path" after six years of meditation and studying. Gautama, upon his awakening, devoted himself to the teaching of the revealed principles and truths of Buddhism. He gave his all to humanity until his passing at 80 years old.

Was Buddha a god?

Gautama did not claim to be a god, nor was he a god. He was a mortal man who discovered the truth through his experience and shared it with others.

Are Buddhists devoted to idol worship?

Buddhists are respectful of images of Buddha. This appraisal is not worship or supplication, but a way to show respect for images of the Buddha. Many Buddha statues depict him with his hands gently resting in his lap, smiling a compassionate smile. This statue encourages Buddhists to find peace and love within themselves. Bowing to the statue does not mean that you are grateful for the Buddha's valuable teachings.

Why do there seem to be two different Buddha representations, one thin and one fat?

It is common to believe that the slimmer and more muscular statues of shirtless men crossed with their legs are both Buddhas. They are not.

Siddhartha Gautama's representation is the image of the slim Buddha. He was considered a medium-sized to slim person because he had spent some time fasting before learning the importance of balance in all aspects.

The statues of the great, giggling Buddha that we see often are not of The Buddha. These images are actually based on a Chinese monk named Ho Tai. Ho Tai was a cheerful monk. Because some Asian languages can't distinguish between the two words, Ho Tai became synonymous with Buddha.

The Buddha is Skinny Buddha. Fat Buddha is either a "buddha", or a monk.

Why is Buddhism so popular in poor countries?

Buddhism teaches wealth is not a guarantee of happiness, and possessions are not eternal. Happiness should not depend on possessions that can be lost. Expensive lifestyles and wealth can lead to attachment. Buddhists can be closer to their nirvana by living simple lives.

It is important that everyone suffers, regardless of their economic status. True happiness can be found in those who are able to understand and incorporate Buddhist teachings into their daily lives. Buddhism doesn't see any problem with wealth as long as it is earned honestly and used for society's benefit.

Is there a different type of Buddhism?

There are many types of Buddhism. Because of cultural differences, the emphasis areas and moral teachings may differ depending on where they are located. The core teaching, the "Dhamma", remains the same.

Are there other religions that are wrong?

Buddhism is open to other religions and beliefs. Buddhism accepts the moral teachings and beliefs from other religions. However, it strives for more. Buddhism offers a realistic and reliable purpose for our long-term existence. It does this by embracing true understanding and wisdom. Buddhism is very open-minded and does not care about labels such as Hindu, Muslim, Christian, Buddhist, etc. Buddhists do not preach their beliefs or try to convert others. If asked, however, they will share their spiritual path.

What are the most significant differences between Buddhism, Christianity, and other religions

Buddhists don't believe in an all-knowing God. They don't believe in an omniscient God. Buddhism is not a religion. Nobody owes any higher power their worship or allegiance. Buddha was not a savior; he was a teacher. He didn't save anyone with his own salvation or enlightenment. He is a guide to all Buddhists, and helps them travel towards happiness and purity. Buddha does not have the power to cleanse sins, or grant forgiveness or salvation. Buddhists don't seek to purify Buddha; they are more interested in following his teachings and purifying their own bodies.

Buddha is nothing else. He was not created in the incarnation of any deity or other unearthly being. He was both a man, a teacher, and Buddhists were his students. Buddhists are responsible for their own liberation from suffering. No one should take credit for their progress, growth, or enlightenment. Buddhists don't follow anyone blindly. Instead, they rely on their own discipline and motivations to think or act in a certain manner. A Buddhist is not saved by immersing themselves in the teachings and texts. This does not necessarily mean they have reached the highest levels. The journey to nirvana is made through the lessons learned from life's experiences.

The teachings of Buddhism will exist regardless of whether Buddha lived or not. Because Buddha discovered and shared these teachings, it is possible to say that he also learned them. They were not written by him and made law. In the hope that others would find their own path to enlightenment, he provided guidance and reflections from his own experience. He is not a prophet.

Buddhism holds that all people have the potential to become Buddhists. This is called Buddha Nature. Enlightenment is possible if someone works hard to learn Buddhism and its teachings. Enlightenment is the ultimate goal for Buddhists. It differs from a desire or a wish to reach heaven or a higher realm.

Karma is one of the fundamental foundations of Buddhist culture. Nothing is eternal and nothing is ever real. There is no divine power that can be created by an authority or sent from the heavens. Buddha's teachings show that there is only the causality and experience of suffering and happiness.

Buddhists believe that all beings and animals should be treated with compassion and loving kindness. Animal sacrifice is prohibited in any way. All sentient beings, including those who live in other worlds, are taken into consideration.

Buddhists are careful not to get attached, even to the idea of doing good or being well. It is considered a craving if they start to see anything as "good", and serve in the name "goodness" rather than enlightenment. Cravings are a form of suffering and another foundation in Buddhism. Every suffering can be analyzed and considered as an obstacle. Sin and suffering do not have to be synonymous. Buddhism doesn't recognize sin. Buddhism does not recognize soul entities. A soul does not belong to one life. It is just that. This doctrine can be found in the Dharma.

Buddhism doesn't negotiate or define the end or beginning of one's existence. There is no beginning cause. Buddhists don't ponder the origin of human existence in general. There are no holy wars in which Buddhists have been included, due to their disinterested in the beginnings of human existence and their precept to not kill.

Transcendent Wisdom is one of the highest positions in Buddhist practice. This is the harmony of emotion, compassion, and logic - it brings together faith and logic. Buddhists believe that meditation is a powerful tool to gain insight. Unfathomable resources can be found within, which will help you on your path to enlightenment.

The cosmology of Buddhism is very different from other religions. It uses the Three Thousand-Fold World System to view the Buddha World and believes there are millions upon millions of solar systems that house millions of beings. Buddhism does not offer eternal damnation or hell. You can only go to a less desirable place. There are many less desirable realms than there are desirable ones.

What's the difference between Buddhism & Hinduism?

Hinduism, unlike Buddhism, is all about discovering the self. Buddhism is about letting go of one's self and thinking, while Hinduism encourages its followers to find deeper understanding.

Hindus achieve success by eliminating physical distractions from their lives. They can focus more on what is inside and themselves without distractions. You will recall that Buddhism doesn't believe in one soul possessing a body, so there is no single entity or person to discover.

Although they are similar in their birthplaces, there are many differences between the two practices. Buddhism does not have any gods or deities. Hinduism is filled with many. Buddhism is about getting rid of ignorance. Hinduism is focused on devotion and good works. While there are many beliefs depending on the sect of Hinduism that you follow, Buddhists believe only in the teachings and values of the Buddha. Hinduism's goal is salvation; Buddhism's goal is enlightenment.

Buddhists follow the Buddha, Dharma, and Sangha. Many Hindus pray three-times a day, at dawn, noon, and dusk. Hindu scriptures tell of a God who chooses those who have done good deeds during their lives. According to the Buddha, Buddhists are responsible in their own enlightenment as well as their attainment of Nirvana.

Traditional Buddhists don't view marriage as a religious obligation. They instead look to the sacred texts for guidance on how to keep a happy marriage healthy and happy. Monogamy is encouraged, as well as loyalty to one's spouse. Many Hindu kings of the past had multiple wives.

You can see that there are many differences between Hindus and Buddhists. Although this list isn't exhaustive, it gives an idea of how vastly different these two belief systems can be.

Is Buddhism Scientific?

Science is based on the observation and testing of facts, and then formulating these into natural laws. This scientific definition of Buddhism is very fitting. Anyone can test and prove the Four Noble Truths to be suitable for their practice. The Buddha asked his followers to verify his teachings rather than blindly accept his wisdom. Buddhism is practical. It relies more on understanding than faith.

What did the Buddha actually teach?

The Buddha was extremely knowledgeable. Many useful lessons were taught by him to humanity. Although the available knowledge is vast, it can be summarized in the Noble Eightfold Path.

The Eightfold Path is the foundation for Buddha's Middle Way. The Middle Way rejects extreme lifestyles, thoughts, actions, and emotions. It's about balance, wandering and cultivating equanimity within the mind and spirit through morality and meditation.

What is the Buddhist ego and what does it mean?

Freud did not describe the Buddhist ego. The Buddhist ego is a collection of mental experiences. These experiences can be divided into five distinct categories (skandhas). These skandhas are a tool for calm, often dispersing panic and confusion. The skandha that first names confusion is actually the skandha called form. Once the confusion is identified, the ego begins to feel about it. If we feel that it is something we enjoy, we want to keep learning about it. We can distance ourselves from it or destroy it if we don't like it. The skandha is the combination of impulse and perception.

Our minds begin to categorize our experiences after we have experienced them. It is part of our human nature to label and give names to the unknown. This helps us to process and plan better. The skandha or concept of understanding what it is will help us to deal with it.

The ego finally experiences the skandha or consciousness. It takes our thoughts and observations, and gives the subject or experience an identity. Because it feels real, we now believe that we understand what something is. Samsara is the process of making sense. The word literally means "to whirl around". Your samsara is the domain that your ego creates.

What are the six realms of existence?

Six realms house all of the infinite possibilities of existence. Buddhism does not view all realms equally. True liberation is possible only in one realm, for instance. The human realm is that realm. The human realm revolves around curiosity, doubt and the pursuit of something better than we currently have. We don't get as obsessed with certain things in this world as we are with other realms. We seek simplicity and the best way of living.

When a mind assumes the animal characteristics of an animal, it is called the animal realm. We are obsessed with making sure our environment is secure and ensuring predictability. We reduce risks and open up new possibilities. Innovation is not possible. Our narrow vision leads to ignorance.

Our ego seeks out a way to have something or someone. We naturally respond to this craving by satisfying it. We want to satisfy our cravings in an endless and compounding way. Consumption becomes a habit. We are in a constant state of craving because we have this desire realm.

The hell realm is a place of deep personal and affecting turmoil. It can trigger our most violent responses, such as anger, frustration, and annoyance. Our negativity is amplified and redirected to make us even more angry. The situation is in a never-ending loop of snowballing and escalating.

The jealous god realm is a form of paranoia that can be characterized as acute paranoia. This is when we become obsessed with other people's perceptions of us. To please others or gain an advantage over them, we act in a particular way. This realm is not trustworthy, but there are many plans for revenge if we ever get slighted.

The god realm is the highest of all six realms. It is entirely imagined. We become complacent and lose sight of the things we once valued. Our confidence begins to erode when we pretend tranquility and then we lose our ability to remain relaxed. Once we realize our inability to relax, we fall into a lower realm. We must complete the cycle: God realm to a jealous god realm; animal realm to a animal realm; animal realm to sex realm; and desire realm to hell realm.

What is wisdom?

Buddhism teaches that wisdom must be developed with compassion and dedication. One could be a kind-hearted fool, while the other could be someone who is devoted to knowledge and avoids emotions. Buddhists seek the "Middle Path" to help them develop both their inner and outer worlds.

To see that all phenomena around you are temporary, incomplete, and don't constitute any fixed entity is the highest level of wisdom. Instead of believing everything we hear, we should seek to understand reality. True wisdom is based on a clear, objective, open and non-bossive mind. To follow the Buddhist path, one must have intelligence, courage and flexibility as well as patience.

What is compassion?

Compassion can be described as empathy, concern, caring, and sharing. Compassion can also be felt as a willingness to comfort others. Buddhism says that you can only understand yourself if you understand others. This can only happen through wisdom development. Once a Buddhist has learned how to overcome suffering, he can help others find the shelter they seek.

He encourages others only to learn after they recognize that they need refuge.

How can I become a Buddhist?

Anyone can understand and test the Buddhist teachings. Buddhism teaches that all solutions to problems can be found within ourselves, not outside. His followers were asked by the Buddha to question his claims. He encouraged them all to verify and test his teachings. People can take responsibility for their actions and thoughts by following Buddhist principles. Buddhism is not a set or regulations that must be accepted. It is an open-ended teaching experience that each person can learn and use in their own ways.

If you are interested in becoming a Buddhist, the first thing you should do is to seek refuge. To find refuge, one must turn to Buddha, Sangha, and Dharma for their teachings. You are a Buddhist if you seek refuge.

The Triple Gem is the combination of the Dharma and Sangha, as well as Buddha, is also known. They are considered to be as valuable as any jewel due to their rarity and significance to the Buddhist belief system. It is possible to feel confident and recognize the Triple Gem as a guide to purification, happiness, and enlightenment. It is evident that Buddha's methods can be learned if one approaches Buddhism with curiosity and openness.

Chapter 15: Meditation

Although there are many ways to meditate in Buddhism, all of them can be referred to as bhavana. Bhavana, an outdated teaching, is not recommended. It is located in the reach of the authentic Buddha who lived more than 25 centuries ago.

Legally, Bhavana, or the Buddhist Buddhist form of meditation is mental culture. It purifies the brain from unsettling influences such as lecherous cravings and disdainful desires, slothfulness and stress, as well as developing such qualities like fixation, mindfulness and knowledge.

Buddhism requires that its followers understand the world and each other in a profound, changing way. If they succeed, they will be "stirred" (buddha). This is what Buddhism uses to achieve it. It was a Hindu tradition, and Buddha used reflection to attain edification.

Over the centuries, Buddhism has developed many systems such as care, adoring consideration and perception. An expert reflection educator can share specific systems according to individual needs.

Different schools of Buddhism use reflection in different ways. A mantra that is repeated to center the brain in a Tibetan convention may be used by meditators. It can also be used in a Buddhist instruction. Care may be achieved in a Theravada convention by focusing on the breath, body and sentiments or the current of thoughts that travels through the mind as the meditators watch and observe themselves. It is important to remember that contemplation does not just bring you quiet.

What is Meditation?

Many things are beyond our control. It is possible to take responsibility for changing one's outlook and accept liability. This is what Buddhism says is the most important thing we can do. It is also the best antitoxin for the anxiety, perplexity, nervousness, scorn and discontent that plagues the human condition.

Meditation, or reflection, is a way to change your psyche. Buddhist reflection practices empower and inspire focus, clarity, enthusiasm, and an unmistakable understanding of the true way of things. Connecting with a particular reflection helps one to see the potential for positive change in the psyche. These quiet, centered perspectives can be transformed into peaceful and stimulating perspectives with patience and teach. These encounters can have a transformative effect and help you to see the bigger picture.

Over the centuries, many contemplation hones have been made in the Buddhist tradition. Although they are all referred to as "mind-trainings", they employ a variety of strategies. Each one is a way to develop a calm and positive outlook.

Meditation: Learning how to meditate

A large number of people learn reflection with the Triratna Buddhist Community. Two essential reflections are shown that were first taught by the verifiable Buddha. This helps to build up the characteristics that are calmness and optimistic positivity, the Mindfulness of Breathing (Metta Bhavana), reflections.

Contemplation is a simple process. However, reading about them is no substitute for learning from a solid and experienced instructor. An educator can give you guidance on how to implement the strategy and how best to handle challenges. Perhaps most importantly, an educator can provide the inspiration and support you need.

Meditation/Reflection: Preparing

You must set up your contemplation position in a casual, yet upright way when you sit down to reflect. This includes sitting on a pad or putting your legs over your head. If this is too difficult, you can sit on your knees or in a chair. You can then close your eyes and feel the sensations. You must be sensitive to what you are experiencing, as this is the thing that will guide your reflections. You can take some time to unwind and sit quietly before you begin a reflection. You might also find some assistance by delicately extending.

What is Meditation important?

One of the most important things that people hear when they hear "Buddhism" is the possibility to contemplate. Although Buddhism is more than contemplation and contemplation aren't unique to Buddhism, it is an important part of Buddhist lessons. You can find entries in Buddhist sacred texts that encourage contemplation and illumination, including the Buddha himself. Many Buddhist sanctuaries offer contemplation classes for all faiths.

To Achieve Enlightenment

One, let's get to the root of why Buddhists think: to attain enlightenment.

Buddhism was not established by some supernaturally chosen prophet or some kind of heavenly divinity but by an individual who understood reality through his own efforts and mental preparation. The future Buddha Prince Siddhartha left the royal residence in search of profound freedom. He then went to study under UddakaRamaputta and Alara Kalama, two of the most respected contemplation educators at the time. The sovereign left his lords to continue taking in more after meeting them in the end.

Later, Sovereign Siddhartha met five monkish lives that practiced self-embarrassment. The ruler decided to leave the group after attempting the technique. He was frustrated by the inability of his brain to develop from the practice of self-humiliation. After six years of looking and practice, Prince Siddhartha was able to fully illuminate himself as the Buddha at age 35. He did this by sitting under a fig tree, a practice he called the "Middle Way."

This is a shallow view, but reflection is not critical to Buddhism. The Buddha achieved illumination through contemplation. Reflection is essential for any person seeking edification. The Buddha did not simply demonstrate that he had achieved edification. He also demonstrated that anyone can do it through reflection. Buddhists do not ruminate to celebrate the Buddha's acknowledgement of reality. They simply acknowledge it firsthand.

The Defilements

The journey to illumination is not the primary reason why Buddhists ponder. In fact, very few Buddhists would even consider ruminating. Many Buddhists think in simple sums. Even if you ponder for 30 minutes a day, it is unlikely that you will be able to grasp the truth of reality in any near future.

Buddhists may not be as interested in the idea of an entire otherworldly world as others, but there are still many reasons to ruminate. In Buddhism, contemplation is one of the main ways to get rid of the three mental pollutants of ravenousness and contempt. These are, in Buddhism, the main cause of all suffering. These contaminations can cause us to suffer from outrage, begrudge and the frustration of not being able to get what we want, as well as the discomfort of having to endure the oddities of the mind. The brain is not only affected by the contaminations. They are also the root cause of our bad deeds. According to Buddhism, this can have negative consequences for us in the future.

A way to combat the debasements in our lives and their negative effects is to improve our psyches through contemplation. Reflection not only improves our lives by preparing our minds to avoid pointless mental endurance, but it also keeps our brains great and healthy for the advancement and improvement of our future lives.

Regardless of the reason one might choose to reflect, contemplation offers many benefits to Buddhists and non-Buddhists. To fully understand contemplation and the reasons why so many people practice it, you need something more than what you can find in books or online. It is similar to playing a sport or an instrument. Contemplation requires practice and cannot be understood by simply reading or clarifying.

It's similar to reading a book about how to play b-ball. Understanding Buddhism is difficult if one doesn't practice it and experience it firsthand. Buddhism, contrary to mainstream belief, is a religion that emphasizes activity.

A popular saying that is widely circulated online captures the essence of Buddhism. It explains why clarity alone cannot fully explain why Buddhists contemplate. Although the adage is not a direct quote from Buddha, it does a good job of summarizing the point.

Chapter 16: Symbolism

Symbolism is used in almost all religions. Many images and objects in Buddhism represent many elements. It is important to understand the meanings of these symbols as well as their concepts. We'll be looking at some of the most popular Buddhist symbols you might encounter on your spiritual journey.

Symbols of Buddha

The Buddha didn't want to encourage veneration so he didn't always accept that he was depicted as an associate to Buddhist practices. The Eight Spoked Wheel was used to represent Buddhism in the early stages. It signifies that the Buddha acts the wheel turner and the wheel is the truth of the law or dharma. There are eight spokes for each step of The Eight-Fold Noble Path.

Another popular image is the Bodhi tree, which is closely linked to Buddha. He was able attain enlightenment under one of these trees.

The Buddha is also represented by Thrones. Siddhartha Gautama (or the Buddha) was born into a family of royal ancestry. The throne is also symbolic of the idea that he is the spiritual ruler and enlightened ruler.

The lion is also a symbol of the Buddha. The practice of Buddhism is known for its strength, power, and regal nature. Therefore, it makes sense that the animal believed to embody these qualities is associated with Buddha.

The footprints of Buddha are often depicted as reminders for his presence on Earth.

Symbols of The Three Precious Jewels

Buddhism is founded upon the idea of the Three Precious Jewels. These three precious jewels are the Buddha, Dharma (or teachings), as well as the Sangha (the community). To symbolize Buddhism, you'll often see three jewels arranged in a triangle.

The Offers

Offerings are a common practice in Buddhism, especially in the East. Each offering has a particular meaning and is used to purify or expel a negative force. These eight fundamental offerings are listed below.

1. Water to clean the mouth/face: This symbolises the idea that positive causes can lead to beneficial results. This offering should be made with clean, fresh, cool and smooth water to symbolize auspiciousness.

2. You can also use water to clean your feet. For this purpose, you should mix water with sandalwood or incense. This combination symbolizes purification. The belief is that if we clean our feet, we can get rid of all negative karma.

3. Flowers. Flowers are a sign of generosity and openness.

4. Incense. The act of lighting light symbolizes discipline and the adhering to moral standards.

5. Light. The giving of light can be interpreted as patience. This can help to dispel ignorance.

6. Perfume can be offered, especially in the form sandalwood and saffron scents. These fragrances are symbolic of perseverance and will help you to find your way to greater understanding.

7. Food. Many foods can be offered that are meant to symbolize the mind.

8. Musical instruments. Many musical instruments are offered to Buddha and other enlightened beings as offerings. Because both sound and wisdom are special powers of mind, they can access phenomena.

There are five Qualities of Enjoyment, in addition to the items mentioned above. These are the mirror, which symbolizes the visual element, and the lute which represents sound. The incense burner for aroma, fruit for flavor, and silk which refers to touch.

Deer

Deer Park, Sarnath was where the Buddha taught his first lesson. His presence is described as so remarkable and his peace so profound that even animals were able to hear him speaking. Two deer were often seen beside the Eight Spoked Wheel in early drawings.

Mountains

A few mountains are of particular significance to Buddhism. Vulture Peak, for example, is where the Buddha appeared multiple times and gave sermons. Mount Meru is the mythological center for the Buddhist universe. It is believed to connect the heavens above the Earth to the hells below.

Each direction also has its own mountain that is sacred to the Bodhisattva. They are:

-Wu Tai Shan of the north

-Pu Tuo Sha, from the east

- Jiu Hua Shan of the south
- Emei Shan of the west

The Buddhist Flag

Many of the symbols that we have described are from ancient history. However, the Buddhist flag is much more recent. Each of the five colors was found in the Buddha's aura when he attained enlightenment. These five colors correspond with specific ideas.

Blue - is a symbol of peace, love and kindness.

Yellow - is the middle. Avoiding extremes.

Red - is the blessing of practice. It represents wisdom, wisdom, dignity and virtue.

White - is the purity of Dharma and the fact it can lead to enlightenment

Orange - Represents the teachings and wisdom of Buddha.

Although symbolism may not be the most important aspect of beginning Buddhism, it is an integral part of the practice's history. It may prove beneficial to learn about the origins of symbols if you're interested in beginning your spiritual journey through Buddhism.

Chapter 17: The Source of Happiness

Happiness is within. Our minds can be at ease when we have a positive outlook and are realistic. When we are kind to others, our happiness will support us no matter how difficult we may face. As Buddha said, if we want to feel happy, we must tame ourselves.

Ordinary Happiness: The Suffering Of Change

Many people view Buddhism as a negative religion, claiming that it identifies all suffering as suffering and doesn't acknowledge happiness. However, this is an inaccurate view. True, Buddhism refers to our normal, everyday happiness as the suffering caused by change. This is because this kind of happiness is not satisfying: it doesn't last and it never gets enough. This is not true happiness. If eating ice cream was true happiness, then we would be happier if we had more of it in one sitting. Soon, however, the joy of eating ice cream turns into sadness and suffering. It is the same with moving to the shade or sitting in the sun. This is the meaning of suffering from change.

Buddhism offers many ways to overcome the limitations of ordinary happiness and the suffering of change so that we can reach the eternal joyous state of being a Buddha. Buddhism explains how to achieve this kind of happiness, despite all the difficulties. This teaching is provided by Buddhism because it holds that everyone wants happiness and that no one wants to feel unhappy. Because everyone wants happiness, and we don't know how to find it, Buddhism teaches us how to get it. Only after that basic level of happiness is satisfied can we move on to deeper and more satisfying levels with advanced spiritual practices.

They have a mind that wants to avoid suffering but they plunge headfirst into it. They wish for happiness but act foolishly and destroy their happiness like a foe.

Also, even though we desire happiness, we don't know how to find it. So, instead of creating more happiness in our lives, we only create more misery and despair.

Happiness is a feeling

There are many kinds of happiness. Let us now focus on the ordinary. We need to understand what happiness is. According to Buddhist thought, happiness can be described as a mental factor. It is an activity that allows us to perceive an object in a particular way. It is one part of a larger mental factor called "feeling", which encompasses a broad spectrum from completely happy to totally miserable.

What is "feeling"? It is the mental element that has the nature of experiencing (myongba). It's the mental activity of experiencing an object, situation, or other situation in a way that makes it an actual experience. We don't experience objects or situations if we aren't feeling happy or sad. Computers process data but don't feel happy or sad. This is what separates a computer from a human mind.

A feeling of happiness or sadness is triggered by the perception of a sensory object. This could be a sight, sound or smell, taste, or a physical sensation like pleasure or pain, or the cognition of an intellectual object, such as thinking about something. It doesn't have to be extreme or dramatic. You can feel very low. It is possible to feel happy or sad at any moment in our lives. Even if we're asleep, it can still be experienced with a neutral feeling.

Definition of Happiness

Buddhism offers two definitions of happiness. The first is defined by our relationship to an object. The second is defined by our relationship with the feeling.

First, happiness is the experience of something satisfyingly. This is based on the belief that it is beneficial to us. Unhappiness refers to the experience of something in a frustrating, unsatisfying way. When something is neither satisfying nor tormenting, we experience it neutrally.

The second definition of happiness is that feeling that, after it ends, we want to be reunited with it again. Unhappiness is that feeling when it arises and we want to get rid of it. A neutral feeling is one that does not have either of these desires.

Both definitions are connected. The way we experience an object in a satisfying manner is when it comes to our minds in a pleasant way. The object is accepted and remains the object of our attention. This means that the object's experience is beneficial to us. It makes us happy and it feels good. We want this experience to continue, and if it ends, we would like it to return. We would use the term "enjoy the object" to describe the experience.

If we have a negative experience with an object, it literally "doesn't come to our minds" (Skt. Amanapa is a pleasant way to experience an object. We don't accept the object, and it doesn't stay as the object in our attention. Our experience with the object is not of any benefit to us. In fact, it is actually hurting us. It should end. We would use the term "not enjoying the object" to describe our feelings about it.

Exaggeration of the qualities of an object

What does it really mean to be comfortable with an object? Comfort with an object means that we accept it as is without being naive or denial of its positive qualities. We now come to the topic of disturbing emotions (nyonrmongs, or Skt). klesha, afflictive emotions; and how they relate to whether an object brings us happiness or sadness.

Lust, attachment, and greed are three of the most disturbing emotions. We exaggerate the positive qualities of an object when we have all three. If we have lust, we are driven to acquire the object. Attachment is a desire to keep the object we have. And greed is a desire for more, even if it's already there. These disturbing emotions can lead us to overlook the flaws of the object. These are not happy states of being, as we don't find the object satisfying. This means that we don't feel satisfied with the object. It is not what it is.

We may feel happy when we see our boyfriend or girlfriend, for example. It is satisfying to be able to see that person. We feel unhappy and dissatisfied when our attachment to the person becomes exaggerated. We don't accept that we are seeing the person right now, and instead want more. We suddenly feel dissatisfaction, uneasiness and unhappiness when we see our loved ones.

Repulsion, anger and hatred are other disturbing emotions. These emotions are characterized by exaggerating the negative aspects of an object, and we want to avoid them if we don't have it. We also want to get rid it when we do have it. When it ends, we don't want it to come back. These disturbing emotions often combine with fear. These emotions are also not happy states of mind because we aren't satisfied with the object. It is not what it is.

We could, for example, be having root canal surgery. Our experience of pain is the object of our perception. We will be happy during the procedure if we accept it as it is. It is possible to have a neutral feeling about the pain. We accept the fact that the procedure will take as long as it takes. And we don't want the dentist to continue drilling. The pain of drilling is not something we feel repulsion, attraction or naivety. We are able to accept it as it is. In fact, the pain of the drilling could cause us to feel happiness because we can prevent future toothache pain.

It is important to remember that just because you are happy with something doesn't mean that you don't want more or less. This is based on your need. This does not mean that we are inactive and stop trying to improve our lives or improve the situation. We can, for example, accept and be satisfied with the progress made in completing a project at work, or recovering from surgery. We can still make progress based on our needs and not be unhappy with the things we have accomplished so far. This is true regardless of how much food we have on our plates or how much money we have in our bank account. If in reality, we don't have enough, we need more. We don't have to exaggerate the negative aspects of being without enough food or money. However, it is possible to make an effort to obtain more food and money without feeling unhappy. It's okay if we succeed. And if we fail, that is also OK. We will manage somehow. But still we try. We try to achieve more without letting our minds wander into unrealistic expectations or worrying about failure.

It was a great example of patience that Shantideva outlined in his chapter (VI.10).

It can be fixed, so why do we get in a bad mood about it? It doesn't matter if it isn't, why get in a bad mood about it?

The Principal Source of Happiness: Constructive Behavior

Constructive behavior is the best way to achieve happiness over the long-term. It means not allowing yourself to be influenced by negative emotions like lust, attachments, greed, repulsion and anger. As the main cause of unhappiness, destructive behavior isn't something you should avoid, it is actually what you do. We might, for example, exaggerate the positive qualities of an object we see in a shop and ignore the legal consequences by stealing it. Anger is when we exaggerate negative aspects of someone else's words and ignore the impact it will have on our relationships.

Being able to act, speak, and think while avoiding disturbing emotions will help you develop the habit of not being affected in the future. If a disturbing emotion occurs in the future, it is best to not act upon it. Eventually, the power of the disturbing emotion may diminish and the emotion will cease to exist altogether. However, the more we react to the disturbing emotions in the future, the stronger they will become.

We have seen that happiness is a state of being able to experience objects without the negative emotions of lust, attachments, greed, repulsion or anger. The object's real nature is accepted as it is without exaggerating its positive or negative points. This is how we experience things. It comes from the habitual practice of constructive behavior. We act, speak and think in a way that accepts the true nature of people, things, or situations.

Chapter 18: Prominent Buddhist Figures

The Dalai Lama

The Dalai Lama, the Tibetan Buddhist sector's chief monk, is responsible for all aspects of Buddhism. The governance of Tibet is traditionally entrusted to the Dalai Lama. This changed in 1959 when China took control of Tibet. The Tibetan capital Lhasa was the Dalai Lama's official residence before the Chinese invasion.

The Dalai Lama belongs to the Gelugpa Buddhist practice in Tibet. This community is the largest and most important in Tibet. In fact, the Dalai Lama was only established recently. There have only been fourteen Dalai Lama in the entire history of Buddhism. Posthumously, the titles of the 1st Dalai Lamas and 2nd Dalai Lama were bestowed.

According to Buddhist beliefs, the current Dalai Lama represents a reincarnation of a former lama who made the decision to reincarnate once more in order to continue his important tasks and not to move on to the next stage of life. Tuku is the Buddhist name for someone who repeatedly chooses to be reincarnated. Gedun Drub, who was born in 1391 but died in 1474, is thought to be the first tulku. Gendun Gvatso is thought to be the 2nd tulku. The 3rd reincarnation of tulku Sonam Gvatso (1578) received the term Dalai Lama, which means "Ocean of Wisdom". Tenzin Gvatso, the current Dalai Lama is.

Selection Process

The High Lamas of Gelugpa Buddhist Tradition and the government of Tibet have to search for the Dalai Lama's Reincarnation when a Dalai Lama passes away. The High Lamas will begin searching for a boy born around the same time that the Dalai Lama died. It can take up to three years to identify the next Dalai Lama. The High Lamas took 4 years to locate the 14th Dalai Lama.

The High Lamas have a variety of methods to search for the Dalai Lama's reincarnation.

*Dreams. Any of the High Lama can communicate the location or mark of the boy who will be the next Dalai Lama through a dream.

*Smoke. The High Lamas will look at the smoke coming from the crematory to determine the direction it was blowing if the Dalai Lama's body has been cremated. They will use this sign to locate the area affected by the smoke.

*Oracle Lake. Lhamo Lhatso is also visited by the High Lamas. It is a holy lake in the middle of Tibet. They observe the lake as they travel to the center of Tibet and look for signs or visions that will help them find the right direction. Visions from the Oracle Lake helped to determine the home and town for Tenzin Gvatso the current Dalai Lama.

Once the High Lamas have located the boy, they present him with many artifacts to help him prepare for becoming the next Dalai Lama. These artifacts include some belongings of the Dalai Lama, who just died. If the boy chooses artifacts that belonged to the former Dalai Lama, it is considered a strong sign. To determine if the boy truly is the reincarnation, this must be considered along with other indicators and signs.

However, the current Dalai Lama says that the process of choosing the next Dalai Lama is still in flux. It would be valid for 2/3 of Tibetans to request that the process of finding the next Dalai Lama Reincarnation is altered.

Tibet is the only place where the hunt for the Dalai Lama's reincarnation is allowed. Because he was originally from Mongolia, the 3rd Tuku was an exception. The government of China has taken Tibet over. However, the current Dalai Lama asserts that if he ever reincarnates, it will not be in China or any other country that lacks freedom. Surprisingly, the current Dalai Lama stated that he doubts he is reincarnated and suggested that the purpose of Dalai Lama might have been fulfilled. The reincarnation process of the Dalai Lama is likely to continue until Tibet is reunited with its spiritual leader.

Tenzin Gyatso is the fourteenth Dalai Lama

Tenzin Gvatso, who was born in Tibet as Lhamo Dolmo in 1935, was immediately identified as Thubten Gvatso's re-embodiment. The High Lamas spent many years searching for the next Dalai Lama re-embodiment until they came across Lhamo Dhondrub. One instance was when the face the deceased Dalai Lama turned towards the north east. A High Lama also saw the Amdo village from the Oracle Lake. The vision of the High Lama clearly showed a small monastery with three stories and a turquoise roof and golden roof, as well as a home with unusual guttering. This vision was similar to the descriptions of Amdo, Kumbum and the home Lhamo Dhondrub, who was just 3 years old at the time. Although the High Lamas visited Lhamo Doonrub's house, they didn't reveal the reason for their visit. After several days, the High Lamas returned to Lhamo Dhondrub's house with the intention of carrying out the final test to determine if Lhamo is the next Dalai Lama. The Lhamo Dhondrub was presented with a number of items, including a rosary and mala. These items were all previously owned by the Dalai Lama. The Lhamo recognized the items immediately and shouted "They're mine!"

Lhamo Dhondrub, who was just over five years old, was sent to a monastery near his home so that he could begin his formal training. He continued his training with the Lhasa chief monks, the capital of Tibet. In 1950, Lhamo Dhondrub, a 15-year-old boy, was made the Dalai Lama. His instatement occurred during the onset of conflict with China. He continued his studies and training until he reached the age of 25.

Lhamo Dhondrub received the new name Jamphel Ngawang Lobsang Yeshe Tenzin Gvatso. He was elected leader of a nation which was based on traditional maps and was classified as a province in China.

There were many changes in the Chinese political landscape during the 1950 instatement of the Dalai Lama. The Chinese government began to communicate their plans to control Tibet. In March 1929, after nine years of Chinese rule, Tibetans gathered on the streets demanding the end of it. The People's Republic of China troops met the rebel Tibetans forcefully and killed thousands of them.

The Dalai Lama was afraid that China's government would kill him, so he fled to India with thousands of Buddhist devotees. Jawaharlal Naehru, then the Prime Minister of India accepted him. Prime Minister Nehru granted permission to the Dalai Lama for him to establish his Tibetan Government in Exile in Dharamsala. The Dalai Lama, along with other Tibetan evacuees, founded their own society, where they preserved and promoted Tibet's culture, language, religion, and arts. Actually, the current Dalai Lama was the first to travel to the West. His charisma was a great help in attracting enormous support for both Buddhist and Tibetan resistance movements.

In 1989, the Nobel Peace Prize was awarded to the Dalai Lama for his non-violent cooperation with China. He knew that many Tibetans would be willing to fight to regain his leadership position in Tibet.

Thich Nhat Hanh

Thich Nhat Hanh, who is a Zen master, peacemaker, poet, writer, and scholar, is well-known all over the globe. Thich Nhat Hánh is second in popularity among Buddhist teachers, after the Dalai Lama. His books include Living Buddha, Peace is Every Steps, Living Christ and Anger, and The Miracle of Mindfulness, which are all bestsellers.

He was born in 1926, and received his ordinance at the age of 16. He founded the An Quang Buddhist Institute in Vietnam when he was 24. In 1961, he went to America to further his studies and to teach comparative religion at Columbia University and Princeton University. In 1963, he returned to Vietnam as a leader in the peace negotiations of Buddhists.

He founded the Order of Inter-being in 1964 during the Vietnam War. His teachings of Buddha were crucial to combat the violence, discord and hatred that engulfed the entire nation of Vietnam. The Tiep Hien Order was made up of only a handful of committed devotees, who were devoted to the teachings and social work of Engaged Buddhism. The Tiep Hien Order was founded on the Mindfulness Trainings (14 precepts). In 1964, Thich Nhat Hah founded the School of Youth for Social Service with many Vietnamese university students and professors. The School of Youth for Social Service was made up of several youth teams that travelled to rural areas to help rebuild villages after the war bombings.

Thich Nhat Hah fled Vietnam in 1966 to call for peace. He was denied permission to return to Vietnam. Martin Luther King nominated him for the Nobel Peace Prize in 1994. He said that "this gentle Buddhist monk, from Vietnam, was an intellectual scholar with immense intellectual capacity." If he were to apply his ideas for peace to the world, it would be a monument to ecumenism and to world brotherhood.

He was the director of the Peace Delegation of Buddhists at the Paris Peace Talks in 1969. He was also the founder of the UBC, or the Unified Buddhist Church (France), which grew with the creation the Sweet Potatoes meditation center. People began to learn about Thich Nhat Hanh's teachings and the popularity of his followers from around the globe. The Plum Village, located in southern France, was established in 1982 as a meditation center and official residence of the Order of Inter-being. Every year, thousands of people from different religions and countries visit the Plum Village to attend the retreats. The village's permanent sangha, or community, is made up of lay practitioners, monks and nuns.

Thich Nhat Hanh's teachings are notable for their emphasis on integrating mindfulness practice into daily living, engagements with the world, and joy. Mindfulness, for him, is being aware of what's going on in our bodies and the world around us. His teachings center on awareness of one's breath. His students are always reminded by him that every action can be seen as an opportunity to connect with the sacred, regardless of whether it is driving your car or washing your dishes. He encourages us all to stop the internal war within ourselves by calming our minds and returning to the present moment. He said, "If peace is achieved, happiness can be had by all." This will bring about peace in the family and society. Happiness is the only way to happiness.

Chapter 19: Mindfulness

This is the core practice of Buddhism. This is when an individual is conscious of both what is happening externally and internally. Mindfulness can be done anywhere and at any time, unlike meditation. Mindfulness can be described as a state of being present in the moment, with awareness of one's thoughts, feelings, environment, and bodily sensations. It is a way to be aware of what is happening in your life and surroundings without judgment. This is one of the many lessons Buddha taught to heal the mind and soul by letting go.

Mindfulness is the key to creating awareness. Mindfulness is the act of paying attention to all that happens around you and exploring them with an open mind. Mindfulness is a practice that helps people become more aware of their bodies, emotions, and the world around them. Mindfulness teaches us how to live a life that is full of awareness and appreciation. Buddhists define mindfulness as a state of being aware of the true nature and purpose of all things. It helps them live in the present and cope with life.

Mindfulness is an important part of our daily lives. When you incorporate it into your routine, you'll find yourself free. Buddha called mindfulness the direct path to freedom. Living in the moment allows you to let go of future regrets and worries, and allows you to enjoy the present. Because the future is not coming, the past is gone. The present is crucial. To achieve enlightenment, you must focus on the present.

Being present or mindful will allow you to pay attention to what is happening at the moment, whether it's painful, pleasant, or neutral. This should be done without attaching judgements or feelings to any situation. You can transform the way you see the world by being present and aware in the present moment. Because you won't dwell on your regrets or fears, but rather accept the world as it is.

It's easy to become so absorbed in thoughts and worries that it becomes difficult to live. Mindfulness is about taking control of your thoughts and how you see the world. Mindfulness will allow you to let go of tension and negativity over time. This will lead to a greater sense of peace, happiness, and joy.

Mindfulness is also about accepting your thoughts and feelings, without judgment or believing that there are right or wrong. Mindfulness teaches people to not allow outside forces, situations or experiences to determine their happiness and peace. Your happiness should never be compromised. As we have said, life will never be the same as it was, and suffering is just a part. Buddha taught that there is a way to get rid of suffering. The first step towards that goal is opening up and letting go.

Mindfulness is a skill that can help you deal with anxiety, stress and depression. It allows you to be present in the moment and not dwell on the past or worry about the future. This practice has many psychological, physical and emotional benefits. While mindfulness is not the same as meditation, both are tools that can help you gain insight and lead you to enlightenment.

Chapter 20: Four Noble Truths

The foundation of Buddhism also contains the Four Noble Truths. These truths are a hypothesis, with the rest Buddha's teachings supporting it. Buddhism is the process of discovering, realizing, and accepting the Truths.

These Truths include the truth about suffering, the truth about the cause of suffering and truth about the path that will free us from suffering.

The conventional explanation of the Truths is that "life is suffering, it is caused by greed, and suffering ends when you stop being greedy.

The Truths can sound absurd if they are not explained properly, as in the above example. People are often left with negative views of Buddhism and will not learn more.

Many people believe that life is suffering and will have to suffer to become a

Buddhist. Many people believe that Buddhism is not for them.

To help you understand the Four Noble Truths and their relevance to the Buddhist path towards Enlightenment, we will break them down one by one.

1. The Truth About Suffering: A lot of confusion about the truth of suffering stems from the translation from Sanskrit into English. This first truth, as it appears in its original text, contains the word dukkha. You may have remembered from the previous chapters that this can refer to suffering, stress, anxiety, or unsatisfaction. To reduce the negative connotation that the word suffering has, many scholars have removed the word suffering and replaced it with stressful.

Simply put, suffering or stress is something that everyone experiences. Buddha wasn't saying life was horrible. Many of his sermons spoke of different types of happiness. You will notice that stress or suffering affects every aspect of your life.

This applies to all aspects of our lives, including good fortune and happy times.

Buddha also taught that life is dukkha, which means impermanent. You identify yourself as an animated being by the components of a living thing. These include form, ideas and predilections. Because your being will eventually die, it is called dukkha.

2. 2.The Truth About The Cause of Suffering. Like a doctor who wants to heal a patient, Buddha must first discover the cause. Buddhism says that suffering is caused by our thoughts. Our suffering is caused by our minds. Next we'll explore how ignorance and desire can bring about suffering in our lives.

i) Desire: All living things have deep-seated desires or cravings. All of us seek pleasure in our senses, and life itself. Entertainment, food, beauty, money and new things are all important to us. These are only a few of the many things people want, depending on their environment and who they are.

The best food, trips and experiences are not guaranteed to last forever. It soon ends and there's nothing more to do. It is lost in time. All the things we want don't bring us lasting happiness or satisfaction. We are miserable until we have it. It eventually fails, or we are left disappointed once we have it. We often want more after we have gotten what we want. This can lead to greed. Greed can lead us to cheating, lying and stealing in order to obtain what we want. Addictions can result from uncontrolled desires. Anger can result from being prevented from achieving what we desire. Anger can lead to arguments and even fights. Desire can cause all of these things.

iii) Ignorance. To understand why ignorance can lead to suffering, it is a good analogy to look at suffering as the fruit of a tree. The trunk is desire, while the branches are greed and bad thoughts and anger. The root of the tree is ignorance.

Ignorance is not just being ignorant. It's the inability to see the truth. Because people are limited in their knowledge, there are many truths they cannot see. We are not all-knowing beings. We often find ourselves in trouble, and we don't realize the consequences of our actions. We are often in trouble because we don't know what to do. Later, we find ourselves saying "If only I knew this ...".."

History is full of examples of ignorance. People believed that the world was flat for long periods of time. Science has proven that there are lights and sounds that we can't see or hear. Buddhists believe that ignorance will lead to misunderstandings and delusions as long as people continue to be ignorant about the world. Buddhism teaches that the only way to happiness and Enlightenment is to overcome ignorance.

3. The Truth About The End of Suffering: We now know the causes and effects of suffering. The third truth is that suffering can be eliminated. This truth is based on

the fact that suffering and its causes can be changed by changing our mindsets. We can eradicate suffering.

When we're ill, we go to the doctor because we know he will be knowledgeable about the disease and the best ways to get us back to our health. A spiritual advisor can also help you to find the wisdom to end your suffering. It is not enough to know the problem and its cause. To solve the problem, we need to be instructed.

4. The Truth About The Path that Frees Us from Suffering: As you may recall, Prince Siddhartha went from living lavishly with his father to becoming an ascetic who lived the hard life of torturing both his mind and body. He realized that happiness is a path that doesn't allow him to live in such extremes. This was called the Middle Path.

The Middle Path is a way to live a life that is not only free of indulgence, but also free of suffering. Buddha provided a simple formula to help you get rid of suffering. This formula can be used for both mental and physical treatments. This is the Noble Eightfold Path as Buddhists refer to it. We'll be looking at this in detail in the next chapter.

Chapter 21: Noble Truths and How to Interpret Them

According to the teaching, Gautama Buddha discovered these Four Noble Truths as he tried to attain enlightenment by meditation. These four statements are the foundation of all Buddhist teachings. These truths were how the Buddha understood the nature and causes of suffering in his life.

Buddhists seek to understand these truths and then follow the path to end suffering.

The truth about suffering

The First Noble Truth of Life is that it is filled with suffering. This could be physical or mental suffering. Suffering can be described as suffering. Suffering is the root of all human problems.

We see pain everywhere we look. We get sick. We lose abilities. We all eventually die.

All suffering is inevitable, that is the First Noble Truth. These sources of pain will fill your life. These events will continue to happen. You will feel the pain even if they aren't as severe as someone else's.

Only we can bear our sufferings and no one else. For example, if you get a cold, you only feel the aches and discomforts that go with it. We can't take another person's pains and disadvantages and make them our own. They cannot do it for us. Buddha teaches us to accept that suffering is inevitable.

Not only is there bodily pain, but suffering can also be mental. These mental states can cause us to feel sad, lonely, or depressed. We feel suffering when a loved one becomes ill or dies. This is different from any other suffering they might be experiencing.

Every day of our lives, humans experience a wide range of mental grievances and annoyances. Perhaps we find ourselves in the company of someone we don't like. A baby may cry uncontrollably. A baby's needs and desires are what cause it to cry. Teens and children suffer from not being able to get the things or do what they desire.

Adults feel frustrated when they can't pay their bills or don't like their jobs. Mental suffering includes all of these.

Don't mistake all the talk about suffering as a guarantee that happiness is impossible. Buddha also stated that happiness can be found in many areas of our lives. Our lives are full of happiness, such as friendship, family, and health. Happiness is something we can often achieve without sacrificing our health.

All we have to do when happiness is present is to recognize it and take the time to enjoy it. With the help of Buddhist mindfulness, you can make the best of the positive parts of your life.

Buddhists believe in happiness. They just acknowledge that happiness is temporary. Their impermanence doesn't mean that we shouldn't enjoy them as they are.

Happiness is about recognizing the difference between true happiness and temporary happiness.

Some people feel tempted to live sexy and promiscuous lives. These actions can lead to venereal diseases, which can result in suffering. They can also cause pain through misunderstandings or hurt feelings. They can also cause suffering through unintended pregnancies or decisions made regarding an unwanted or unplanned pregnancy.

This does not mean that Buddhists avoid sexuality and sexual practices. It is possible to find happiness through sexual activity. As with all aspects of life, it is important to choose the right actions when dealing with sexual matters.

It is important to see the larger picture and consider the long-term consequences of your actions, rather than focusing on the momentary pleasures.

The Buddha taught that there were four inevitable physical sufferings in life: death, sickness, old age and birth. He also spoke out against three mental sufferings, namely separation from loved ones, contact with people we don't like, and frustration of our desires. He stressed that acknowledging that suffering is part of everyday life is the first step in ending it is the hardest.

The truth about the cause of suffering

The Noble Truth of the Next Noble Truth is to understand the root cause of suffering. Without knowing the root cause of suffering, you cannot solve a problem. This concept of the cause is similar to a doctor diagnosing an injury before treating it. It is an important step on the path.

The Buddha observed people and realized that suffering is caused by two things: 1) cravings or desires and/or 2) ignorance. These are the causes of the Second Noble Truth.

All the things a person might desire in life are called cravings. This could be food, entertainment or the company of certain people. It could also include money, beauty, money, excitement, and other things. It is the desire to feel pleasures or excitement in life that causes suffering.

There is nothing wrong with living life. As we discovered from the First Noble Truth, life and its pleasures are temporary. Many of the causes that bring us happiness can also lead to our suffering.

This is why mindfulness is so important. You can still enjoy a favorite meal if you are mindful of the moment. The moment is not a cause of suffering. The suffering is caused by the desire to eat that same meal again. Good food can bring you happiness, but it is fleeting.

The solution is to not eat too much of the things that give us pleasure. Did you ever eat too many of your favorite foods? You will feel sick if you eat a lot of rich desserts. You may lose interest in eating the same food every day.

It is the same for any sense pleasure, as Buddha taught. Too many of these experiences can lead to boredom or even worse, make you unhappy. These pleasures are not what make you happy.

Ignorance is closely related to cravings. According to the Buddha, our different cravings are like branches on a tree. The roots of the tree are ignorance. In ignorance, cravings can grow. The seeds of desire can also fall wherever there is ignorance.

According to Buddhism, ignorance does not refer to a lack in education or knowledge. Ignorance can also refer to the inability or unwillingness to see things the way they are. Many truths may be hidden in the world because people have limited understanding.

However, this does not mean our knowledge cannot be improved. There have been many advances in our understanding of medicine and astronomy. We have the ability see beyond our ignorance.

We are unlikely to know all the truths of life and will continue to make decisions based on misunderstandings and delusions. These misunderstandings can cause suffering.

We can reduce suffering from ignorance as humans. We can learn and cultivate wisdom within ourselves and in others. You can find truth and understanding by studying, thinking clearly, and meditating. This will lead to happiness.

The truth about the end of suffering

You will be more prepared to recognize the third Noble Truth once you have understood the Second Noble Truth that ignorance and craving are the causes of suffering. The Buddha took many years to find a way to end suffering. He came to the conclusion, however, that this world can end all your suffering.

To end suffering, you must get rid of all desires, ill will, or ignorance. This is the Third Noble Truth.

The Buddha said that if you stop suffering, you will find supreme happiness. This path will lead you to greater joy and a happier life. Buddhism encourages you to walk this path all your life.

Buddhist teachings say that happiness can be achieved regardless of the circumstances. It is possible to be surrounded with people who have cravings or desires. It is possible to be surrounded with anger and ill-will. You can still live happily and not be influenced by these emotions.

It is possible to not end your suffering immediately. It's okay. There are no deadlines. It is important to practice

Buddhism every day. It's okay to fail. Keep practicing.

Buddhism's concept of Enlightenment is the end of suffering. The ultimate and final goal of Buddhist practice is Enlightenment. But what exactly is this?

Enlightenment can be described as the removal of all suffering and a release.

Enlightenment is a state of mind that enables one to be both wise and compassionate. This is possible by letting go of ignorance and cravings. Wisdom and compassion of the enlightened person will result in less suffering for others and help them to overcome their own suffering.

It is possible to attain enlightenment in this lifetime. It is not something you can attain after your death.

The truth about the path to suffering relief

We finally reach the discussion about the Fourth Noble Truth. This truth is what reveals the path to end suffering. This path is known as the Middle Path in Buddhism.

Gautama Buddha lived a life of extreme wealth, luxury and pleasure. He also experienced extreme poverty, hunger and suffering. He learned that neither extreme was the best way to live. The Middle Path is the Buddhist path that avoids extremes.

According to the Buddha's Middle Path, happiness is found in a moderate lifestyle. The path to enlightenment requires that you avoid both indulgences and denial.

Buddhism requires that one not seek endless pleasures in order to practice it. However, it is important to not cause yourself pain or suffering by ignoring your needs. Not putting yourself in situations where you are lacking will lead to more happiness. It can be hard to find the Middle Path. That is why Buddhism is sometimes referred to as a "practice". It takes practice.

The Buddha provided a guide to help you follow this path. It's called the Noble Eightfold Path. The Noble Eightfold Path will be covered in a later chapter. However, its components are as follows.

Right understanding

Right attitude

Right speech

Right action

Right livelihood

Right effort

Right mindfulness

Concentration is key

These guidelines will be explained in greater detail in the chapter entitled "The Noble Eightfold Path: What Does It Mean?"

You should know that this path will lead to less suffering. This path fosters wisdom and compassion. It is a path that creates good karma, which makes the world a better place to live in.

Conclusion

I hope that you have received a lot of answers to your questions about Buddhism after this segment. You might have also realized that the primary purpose of the First Buddha was to assist others.

Practicing the lessons in your daily life is the best way to make the most of them.

All things considered, Buddha himself stated that walking the path of Buddhism is the best way to understand it.

It is not unusual to depart from the path that the Buddha has so consciously urged one to follow. This is especially true in today's world filled with desires and diversions.

These are some suggestions to help you keep practicing what you've just adapted each day.

Start every day with a prayer of intention. To develop thoughts of cherishing thoughtfulness, create a morning mantra you can gently announce to yourself each morning.

The second is to make a time for contemplation every day with yourself. It is similar to finding the perfect place to eat your meals that you set aside time to care for your soul and psyche. Perhaps the best time to start contemplation is right after you wake up in the morning. Try it out and see how it changes your day.

The third is to remind yourself of the fundamental principles of Buddhism every day. Sometimes it can be difficult, especially if your brain is full of obligations.

It all starts with you letting go of the idea that "I would rather not damage anyone with my thoughts, words, or activities." You will be more conscious of your choices and likely to choose the best. The last thing you should do is take a few minutes at the end of each day to practice caring.

This is the time most people feel least tired and energized. It is a great time to reflect on the day and learn from it.

This could help you discover more about yourself. These are just a few of the many ways you can incorporate the teachings of Buddha into your daily life. Take your time and approach it with care.

www.ingramcontent.com/pod-product-compliance
Lightning Source LLC
Chambersburg PA
CBHW071845080526
44589CB00012B/1116